Liquid Polymer Clay

Ann Mitchell and Karen Mitchell

Published by

krause publications
An F&W Publications Company

700 East State Street • Iola, WI 54990-0001
715-445-2214 • 888-457-2873
www.krause.com

Please call or write for our free catalog of publications. Our toll-free number to place an order or obtain a free catalog is 800-258-0929, or please use our regular business telephone 715-445-2214.

All photography by Cristopher Lapp, www.cristopherlapp.com
Edited by Jodi Frazzell
Book design by Marilyn McGrane

Library of Congress Catalog Number: 2003101339

ISBN: 0-87349-563-2

Dedication

This book is dedicated to our mother, Annamarie Mitchell, for sharing her talents and love of crafts with us.

Acknowledgments

We would like to express our appreciation for the support and generosity of the following people and companies:

Esther Anderson
Shelley Crossen
Kathleen Dell'Orto
Carol Duvall
Erinn Eichinger
Cam Frierson
Gwen Gibson
Sue Heaser
The Leather Factory
Kari Lee
Margaret Maggio

Wayne Marsh
Barbara McGuire
Steen Mitchell
Hope Phillips
Polyform Products
Nan Roche
Marie and Howard Segal
Jezra Thompson
Pier Voulkos
Jan Walcott

With special thanks to:

Cristopher Lapp
Ai Buangsuwon
Randy Townsend
Mitch Buangsuwon
Alex Buangsuwon

Thank you to all of our wonderful customers who have supported us for years.

Table of Contents

Chapter 3: Basic Applications and Techniques 20

Chapter 4: Tips . .36

Chapter 8: Surface Decoration 94

Chapter 9: Glass Effects 112

Introduction

Think outside of the box. This is the creative philosophy we follow in our continued exploration of polymer clay. Inspired by the possibility of a new direction in polymer clay, we began experimentation with liquid polymer clay upon its availability to the craft market. From this, we have developed exciting new techniques.

Liquid clay: It is white. It is gooey. What do you do with it? This book offers you an overview of liquid polymer clay, along with some of our techniques. Throughout the book, the liquid polymer clay is applied to a variety of other materials, expanding on the concept of mixed media art. Historically and culturally developed concepts influence many of the techniques in this book. Each project chapter outlines the evolution of these concepts in art and provides sources of inspiration that lead to the approach in clay.

As with any new art material, many artists forge ahead along similar paths as the material allows, and parallel development of techniques sometimes occurs. The ideas presented here are the result of our own extensive exploration with liquid polymer clay. We have applied our techniques to many types of objects, using our own inherent creative style. Examples of these pieces can be seen in the Gallery of Ideas at the end of every project chapter. The galleries are meant to inspire each individual to learn the techniques and to apply it to an object in their own area of interest. These visual images are offered as a jumping off point, and we ask that each artist add their unique style in order to create original works.

Get your hands dirty. The best way to understand a new material is to try it out, so do not hesitate to jump in and try this art material to see where it takes you. Have fun!

ANN AND KAREN

Chapter 1

Working With Solid and Liquid Polymer Clay

Solid Polymer Clay

Polymer clay is a flexible, easy to use modeling clay that comes in a wide range of colors. Each brand has a slightly different formulation, so the individual characteristics of the clay will vary between brands. The projects in this book have all been made with Premo. Although Premo can get rather sticky in warmer climates, it is a clay that is easy to condition and shape, and bakes to a good strength with some flexibility. It is important that you work with the clay you are most comfortable with; experimentation is encouraged.

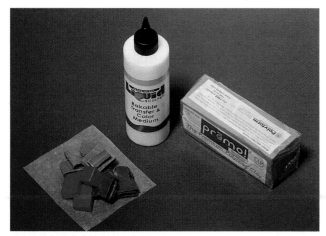

Samples of solid and liquid clays.

Picture frame, necklaces, and bracelet that utilize clay fabric as links between the solid polymer clay elements.

Handling

As with any art material, attention to careful handling of the polymer clay is recommended. Those with sensitive skin or concerns regarding clay residue, should use gloves or a barrier hand cream for hand protection. Hands should be washed before and after handling clay. Do not eat near your clay work area, as you want to avoid getting crumbs in the clay, as well as avoid ingesting clay residue. The clay itself should not be eaten. Tools, cutters, surfaces, and ovens used for clay should not be used for food. Clay should be kept away from food preparation and consumption areas.

Work surface

It is important that you have a work surface for clay that is smooth, compatible with polymer clay, resistant to cutting tools, and easy to clean. Some good work surfaces for both solid and liquid polymer clay are granite, marble, glass, ceramic tile, and acrylic. Wax paper can be placed between the work surface and the clay to prevent sticking and provide easy release of the clay from the surface.

Conditioning

All types of solid polymer clay require some conditioning before use. Conditioning consists of rolling and blending the clay to increase its softness and workability, and to re-mix the plasticizers in the clay for increased strength after the clay is baked. Softer clays in small quantities can be conditioned by hand. For harder clays or larger amounts of softer clays, squeezing and hand rolling clay with an acrylic rod or brayer may not be adequate for full conditioning. Passing the clay repeatedly through a clay-designated pasta machine is one of the most effective means for quickly conditioning clay. If you plan to work with polymer clay on a regular basis, it is a good idea to invest in a pasta machine. The Atlas brand is the most popular, and is the brand used in this book. Having a pasta machine will cut down on the stress to hands and wrists that can occur during clay conditioning, and it can also speed up the process. For harder clay such as Fimo Classic, a clay-designated food processor for initially chopping the clay may be helpful. Both solid (Fimo mix quick) and liquid (Sculpey diluent) clay softeners are available to aid in the conditioning process, but they should be added gradually in small amounts.

To condition a softer clay such as Premo, first unwrap a block of clay and slice off pieces slightly thicker than the thickest setting of the pasta machine. Next, roll each slice through individually, and then stack the sheets and roll again repeatedly, making sure not to trap air between the layers. Rolling the clay through the pasta machine at a slightly thinner setting can speed up the conditioning process. When folding clay sheets to run through the pasta machine, always place the fold towards the rollers or to the side, as this is one way to prevent trapping air bubbles. When the clay does not crack at the edges if run through the pasta machine and is pliable enough to handle easily, you are ready to start your project. If you leave a piece of clay resting for a few days, it may require some additional conditioning. Do not over condition your clay to the point of stickiness. If this occurs, allow the piece of clay to rest overnight.

Color mixing

Mix colors by first conditioning the individual colors, measuring the amount desired of each color, and then mixing the two together completely. If a precise color mix is not required, the colors can be mixed during the initial conditioning process.

Storage

It is important that you keep your clay wrapped or in sealed soft plastic containers to prevent slow hardening of the clay and contact with dust particles. By wrapping clay in wax paper and then setting it into a soft plastic sealed container, or by storing it in self-sealing plastic bags and then placing it in a cool (but not cold), dark place, you can prolong the shelf life of your clay. Excess heat can cause the clay to harden (especially if you leave it in your car), and improper wrapping can cause the clay to slowly harden and lose flexibility.

Baking

For best results, bake solid polymer clay according to the manufacturer's directions. Time and temperature may vary slightly between clay brands. In general, it is important not to bake any polymer clays at a temperature higher than recommended, as it may cause the clay to burn and emit potentially harmful fumes. Translucent clays are especially sensitive to temperature, and they may brown if not baked carefully with good temperature control.

You will need an oven, preferably one designated for clay baking. It may be a good idea to purchase an inexpensive toaster oven or convection oven if you intend to do a lot of clay baking. A toaster oven does not blow around the hot air inside the oven as a convection oven does, so it will limit the amount of fumes emitted. Some artists feel that a convection oven holds a steadier temperature, so oven selection may be based on personal preference. For the best ventilation, place the oven outside while baking. If you live in a cold or wet climate, it may be necessary to place the oven under cover from rain. Bring the oven indoors when it is not in use. Another solution for better ventilation is to keep a fan in your work area and to leave the windows cracked open to blow the fumes out of your work space. You will need oven mitts to protect your hands and an oven thermometer to check the consistency of temperature, especially in the smaller ovens. For best results, preheat the oven to assure an even temperature. While clay is baking, leave the oven closed to maintain the steady temperature. If clay has

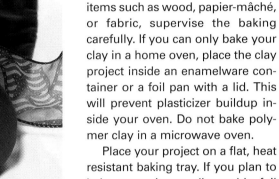

been attached to heat sensitive items such as wood, papier-mâché, or fabric, supervise the baking carefully. If you can only bake your clay in a home oven, place the clay project inside an enamelware container or a foil pan with a lid. This will prevent plasticizer buildup inside your oven. Do not bake polymer clay in a microwave oven.

Place your project on a flat, heat resistant baking tray. If you plan to bake many items, disposable foil trays offer an inexpensive option for having multiple trays to rotate. Lining the trays with parchment or wax paper will make for easier removal of the projects from the trays. Placing items on wax paper may cause shiny spots on the bottom of projects. Smaller items can be baked on index cards, as long as baking is supervised. Foil, skewers, folded heavy cardstock, and polyester batting are all effective materials for propping up hard to bake items. Curved clay items may need support in order to hold their shape during the baking process. Fresh out of the oven, solid clay will be quite flexible, so it is important to cool it first on the support material before completing your project. After baking, flat sheets of clay should be placed under a heavy object or book while still warm (protect the book with wax or parchment paper) to keep them flat while cooling. When you remove a baked clay item from the oven, stand away from the oven and do not inhale the fumes being emitted. If, for any reason, your clay becomes overheated and starts to smoke or burn, do not open the oven. Turn off and unplug the oven, and leave the oven door shut until it cools completely. If you are baking indoors, open all the doors and windows and exit the room until the fumes have dissipated.

Finishing

Polymer clay will have a matte finish after baking, which can be left alone or finished in a number of ways. Solid clay can be wet sanded with fine grit wet/dry sandpapers, readily available at auto parts supply stores. Progressing from a 400 to a 600 and then an 800 grit sandpaper followed by buffing will result in a smooth sheen on the surface of the clay. Wet sanding and rinsing the project is important, as it prevents inhaling airborne particles of clay dust (you can also wear a dust mask). Once the piece is sanded, it can be buffed with a cloth or a buffing wheel. Wearing protective goggles is essential, especially when buffing. The combination of sanding and buffing is an effective method for removing fingerprints from flat (non-dimensional) clay projects, but it is not good for dimensional clay surfaces. For a beautiful sheen on dimensional pieces, several coats of a polymer clay varnish are a nice alternative. The Fimo gloss finish polymer clay varnish (not water-based) produces the most attractive finish. This will require application with a brush in a ventilated area, and you will need brush cleaner. Some artists use the water-based Flecto Varathane Diamond Wood Finish as a clay finish. Spray finishes should not be used, as many will leave a tacky surface on the clay, especially over time.

Clean up

To remove clay residue from skin, first use a baby wipe or hand lotion, and then wash with soap and water. Special heavy-duty hand cleaning soaps can aid in this process. Always wash your hands before and after coming in contact with polymer clay. It is also essential that you keep your work surface clean, to prevent dust particles from getting stuck in the clay, and to avoid spreading clay residue around your studio or workspace. Your work surface, tools, and pasta machine can be cleaned with a paper towel dampened by isopropyl alcohol. The alcohol will remove the residue, and it dries quickly so it will not cause your tools to rust. It is also a good idea to clean the pasta machine often and between colors to prevent spreading the previous color to the new color.

Liquid Polymer Clay

There are several brands of liquid polymer clay currently available. The first, manufactured by Polyform, is called Liquid Sculpey and is available in both a translucent and a white color. Due to both availability (at the time of project development) and consistency in performance, all of the projects in this book have been done with Translucent Liquid Sculpey. Another version, Kato Clear Polyclay Medium, is relatively new and has been tested more recently with the applications and techniques discussed in this book. You will find comparisons in texture and performance of both the Liquid Sculpey and the Kato Polyclay Medium listed with each application and technique discussed in the next chapter. Translucent Liquid Modelene is a brand available in Australia. It was not tested for this book. As with the solid clays, experimentation with a variety of brands of liquid clay is encouraged, as they will perform differently depending on the application. Below you will find a list of the basic properties of Translucent Liquid Sculpey and Kato Clear Polyclay Medium.

Translucent Liquid Sculpey:
- Milky white before baking
- Sticky yet viscous texture before baking
- Bakes to a matte finish
- Some odor before and during baking, stronger than solid polymer clay
- Effective clay-to-clay adhesive
- Translucent yet slightly frosted look when baked in thin sheets and with transfers
- Self leveling
- Molds easily in thin applications

Kato Clear Polyclay Medium:
- Milky white before baking
- Runny and somewhat sticky texture
- Bakes to a satin (shiny) finish
- Strong odor before and during baking
- Effective clay-to-clay adhesive
- Very clear look when baked in thin sheets and with transfers
- Not self leveling, uneven baked surface with thin molds

Polyform Products first developed Liquid Sculpey in the early 1970s. The original purpose of the liquid form of this clay was for manufacturing of buttons, magnets, and jewelry (the prototypes that were first made in Sculpey). Oven cured in silicone rubber molds, the liquid clay items could be easily removed from the molds when cool. Initially, the clay was available in an array of colors, and it was often enhanced with acrylic paints after curing. Some companies used the liquid clay to make large quantities of reproductions of original designs. The liquid clay was reformulated more recently to accommodate the requests of artists seeking a less viscous form of the clay to create surface decorations on their projects. Currently, the translucent version of the Liquid Sculpey is the most readily available, and it can be easily tinted to the artist's color of choice.

Handling

Translucent Liquid Sculpey has a milky white appearance, and it is viscous yet somewhat sticky. It bakes to a smooth matte finish. If baked on glass, liquid clay can achieve a high gloss finish on one side. Kato Clear Polyclay Medium is thinner in consistency than Liquid Sculpey, and it bakes to a somewhat clearer shiny finish. Because of the slightly sticky and viscous nature of liquid polymer clay, extra care should be taken in handling. The same guidelines suggested for handling of solid polymer clay apply to the liquid form (refer to handling instructions, page 10).

Work surface

In addition to the work surfaces discussed for solid clay, you will need a piece of glass for many liquid clay applications. It is a good idea to find one that both fits into your baking tray and is large enough to work on. A piece of glass from an old picture frame will work, just be aware of the sharp edges. If you cover the edges, do so with a material that is resistant to the heat in the baking process.

Conditioning

Since the clay is already in liquid form, it does not require conditioning. Liquid Sculpey will thicken over time, even when stored in sealed containers, so it may be necessary to thin the clay for some applications. In this case, the best option for thinning the clay is Sculpey diluent, produced by Polyform and specially formulated as a clay thinner (and softener for solid clay). The diluent should only be added one drop at a time and then mixed into the amount of clay you are using for the project. It only requires a very small amount of diluent to change the texture of the clay. If you plan to color your liquid clay, add color first and then thin it with diluent if necessary, as the texture will change depending on the colorant you choose. If you wish the clay to thicken, place it in a polymer-clay-compatible container, loosely covered with plastic wrap or wax paper for several days to weeks.

Color mixing

All brands of liquid polymer clay are most readily available in a translucent color. This is a versatile option because it can be used as an invisible adhesive, and it can also be tinted to any color with a variety of materials and used for surface decoration. The two most effective colorants for liquid clay are mica pigment powders and oil paints.

Mica pigment powder comes in a wide range of shades, and it will give the liquid clay a beautiful metal-lic or pearlescent sheen in addition to rich color. The mica powders should be added a small amount at a time, often even $1/16$ teaspoon is an adequate amount to tint $1/2$ to 1 teaspoon of clay. If a richer color is desired, add another small amount of mica, mixing the powder in completely between each addition. If you add too much powder, the liquid clay will turn into a paste. You can thin this paste by adding more liquid clay or a drop of diluent. Adding too much powder may cause the liquid clay to lose strength and flexibility in thin sheet applications.

Oil paint offers the option of giving the liquid clay a sheer vivid color tint without a pearlescent sheen and without thickening the clay. In fact, the addition of oil paint will thin the liquid clay slightly. For a light tint, a dot of oil paint (just what fits on the end of a skewer) is enough to tint $1/2$ teaspoon of translucent clay. For a deeper color, a dab the size of half of a pea is adequate to color $1/2$ teaspoon of liquid clay. A wooden skewer is an excellent tool for adding color and mixing the clay; just make certain to wipe the skewer with a paper towel between each color. As with mica powder, add more color sparingly, mixing thoroughly each time.

To create an opaque color for a glaze, first make the translucent clay opaque by adding in a dab of titanium white oil paint, and then tint the white clay. Mica powders and oil paints can be used together to make one color. The combination will create a balance in the texture between thick and thin liquid clay, and it will produce a bright color that has sparkle. Other materials can be used to tint your liquid polymer clay. These include artist's pigments and coal powder. Both of these will have a slightly

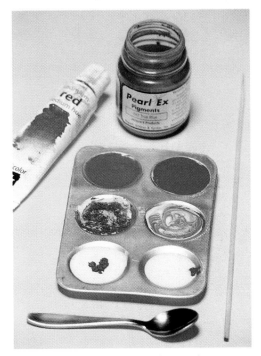

Color mixing with oil paint and mica powder.

grainy effect, but they can produce exceptionally rich colors. Numerous inclusions can add both color and texture to the liquid clay. Some options for inclusions are glitter, metal powders, embossing powders, dried plants and flowers, tiny beads, mica flakes, metallic leaf flakes, bits of paper, fabric, lace, and sand. When using any type of powdered pigment, it is a good idea to wear a dust mask to avoid inhaling airborne particles. Whenever using liquid clay tinted with powdered pigments, it is important to stir the pigments in completely before each use, as the powders may settle over time.

Liquid polymer clay should not be tinted with acrylic paint, as the water base in the paint will cause steam and bubbles to form during baking, making a rough texture in the liquid clay. Concentrated watercolor inks can be used to tint liquid clay, but they will cause minute bubbling in the clay.

Colored pencils (not watercolor), such as Walnut Hollow or Prismacolor brands, and oil pastels work well for tinting photocopy transfers made with liquid polymer clay. The colors will change in the transfer process, so it

Right:
Colored pencils and test strips.

Below:
Items used to tint liquid clay.

is a good idea to create a color test strip for your chosen brand of pencils or pastels in order to yield consistent results in your projects (refer to transfers, page 25).

Storage

As mentioned earlier, Liquid Sculpey will thicken over time, even in a sealed container. Liquid polymer clay can be stored in metal, glass, wax-coated paper cups, or flexible plastic containers. The plasticizers in the material will react with hard plastic or craft foam. For long-term storage, baby food jars with tight lids will work well. For storing small amounts of tinted clay, aluminum containers with glass lids are ideal. Always cover your liquid clay to avoid excess thickening and to prevent dust from getting stuck in the clay. As with solid clay, you can prolong the life of your liquid polymer clay by storing it in a cool dark place in a tightly sealed container or in its original bottle (place upright to prevent leakage). For projects in progress, small glass dishes or aluminum palettes work well, and they can be covered with wax paper or plastic wrap for short periods of time.

Baking

The same guidelines that apply to baking solid polymer clay also apply to liquid polymer clay (refer to baking, page 11). The recommended temperature for baking liquid polymer clay is 275–300 degrees (F). Although the translucence is better when baked at the higher temperature, it is often a good idea to bake your liquid clay at 275 degrees (F). Many liquid clay projects are done in combination with the solid polymer clay, which is more safely baked (for most brands) at 275 degrees (F). This temperature will produce good results with both the solid and the liquid clay, and it avoids the risk of burning or discoloring your project. A few projects in this book require a slightly lower temperature of 265 degrees (F), as will be indicated in the directions. The special temperatures relate to baking safety and project results. It is important to have a good oven thermometer to ensure proper baking for both liquid and solid polymer clays. The recommended time for baking liquid clay is 15 to 30 minutes. The length of time has been shortened in many projects due to the project being baked numerous times.

When baking on glass, whether it is a baking surface or the base of the project, the glass needs to be handled carefully. Hot glass should be placed on a heat resistant surface when removed from the oven, but not metal or stone. The sudden temperature change of putting hot glass on a cool surface can cause the glass to crack. If you are applying liquid clay to glass, it is important to cool the glass completely between applications, or the hot glass will cause a fresh layer of clay to bake upon contact, making the surface lumpy. If you are baking clay onto metal, watch your project carefully during baking, as the metal will heat up quickly, and it may raise the temperature of your project while baking. If you are baking clay on wood, it is a good idea to preheat the oven to 265 degrees (F), and bake the unfinished wood first for 20 minutes. After the wood has cooled, clay can be added. Pre-baking the wood will eliminate some of the moisture that can produce bubbling in the clay. Some bubbling may still occur, and with liquid clay this can be used as a textural design element.

Finishing

Similar to the solid clay, Liquid Sculpey will have a matte finish after baking. Kato Polyclay Medium will have a shiny finish. Baked liquid clay can be wet sanded and buffed (refer to finishing for solid clay, page 12). The liquid clay is more difficult to sand. It may require more effort for a strong sheen. The Fimo gloss finish varnish (not water based) is an excellent way to enhance the sheen and translucence of the liquid clay. In some instances, varnish is necessary to achieve the desired glass-like effect for several of the projects in this book.

Clean up

Because of the sticky viscous nature of the liquid polymer clay, you will need to clean your work surface and tools more often than you would with solid polymer clay. When cleaning a metal palette or glass dish that has been used for mixing clay, first wipe the container out thoroughly with a dry paper towel, and then remove the residue by wiping the container again with a paper towel dampened with isopropyl alcohol. To remove liquid clay from your hands, first wipe your hands with a dry paper towel, followed by a baby wipe or hand lotion, and then finish by washing your hands with a heavy-duty soap. To remove liquid polymer clay from a brush, wipe the brush first with a dry paper towel and then with a paper towel dampened with isopropyl alcohol. Repeat this process until the bristles are no longer sticky. Make sure to dry the brush completely before using it again with liquid clay, so as not to contaminate the clay.

SAFETY REMINDERS

- Make sure to use a work surface to protect your table top.
- Do not eat or store food near your polymer clay.
- Do not use the same work surface, tools, cutters, or oven (if possible) for food and clay.
- Wash hands thoroughly before and after using the clay.
- Clean hands with a baby wipe or lotion before washing with heavy-duty soap to remove the excess clay residue.
- Use gloves or a barrier cream if you have sensitive skin.
- Do not eat the clay.
- Clean tools and work surface regularly with isopropyl alcohol.
- Store solid clay in sealed plastic bags or PVC-friendly sealed plastic containers.
- Store liquid clay in sealed glass, metal, or PVC-friendly containers or the original bottle.
- Use an oven thermometer to monitor baking temperature.
- Use oven mitts for removing the baking tray from the oven.
- Use a safe non-flammable baking surface.
- Supervise baking carefully when it involves glass, metal, papier-mâché, or wood elements in combination with the solid or liquid clay.
- Keep a fire extinguisher in your work area.
- Do not inhale baking fumes.
- Bake in a well-ventilated area, preferably outside.
- If your clay smokes or burns, do not open the oven door. Turn off the oven and open doors and windows.
- Wear safety goggles when finishing and buffing clay.
- Wet sand the clay to keep from creating airborne clay particles that can be inhaled.
- Wear a dust mask for sanding and while using any type of powdered pigments.
- Cool any glass baking surface slowly to prevent cracking of the glass.
- Use varnishes and adhesives in a well-ventilated area.

ONCE YOU HAVE A BASIC UNDERSTANDING OF THE PROPERTIES AND HANDLING PROCEDURES FOR BOTH SOLID AND LIQUID POLYMER CLAY, YOU CAN EXPLORE THE COUNTLESS PRACTICAL AND CREATIVE APPLICATIONS FOR THESE EXCITING MATERIALS.

Chapter 2

Tool Kits

O nce you have achieved an understanding of solid and liquid polymer clays, their properties, and handling methods, the next step is to assemble a tool kit. In this case, you will need several tool kits, which will be outlined in this chapter. From there, you can start to try some of the basic applications of liquid polymer clay.

For both solid and liquid clay, the first tool kit you need for any project is for baking. A basic tool kit, which includes the necessities for working with solid polymer clay and some tools also used in jewelry making, follows this. The third kit lists the items needed for working with liquid polymer clay.

The extra tool kit, jewelry findings kit, and adhesives kit are not listed in any specific project. These items have been grouped as kits to aid in organizing your work space. Items from these three kits are listed individually in the projects as needed.

Baking kit

- Oven, preferably a clay-dedicated toaster or convection oven
- Enamelware lidded roasting pan or lidded foil pan for use with home oven
- Flat heat-resistant baking tray, as big as will fit in your oven
- Oven thermometer for careful temperature regulation
- Oven mitts to protect your hands from heat
- Timer to ensure proper baking time

Basic tool kit

- Your hands
- Work surface such as granite tile (shown here), marble, glass, ceramic tile, or acrylic
- Cutting tools
  - Tissue blade or Sculpey slicer for thin cuts
  - Kato NuBlade (Prairiecraft) for slicing thicker slabs of clay and long cuts
  - X-acto or craft knife for detailed cutting
  - Scissors for cutting out patterns, mosaic tiles, fabric, and trims
- Rolling tools
  - Pasta machine (Atlas brand recommended for frequent use)

- Brayer (acrylic or hard rubber) or an acrylic rod for adhering sheets and rolling small pieces of clay
- Basic jewelry tools for jewelry and mixed media clay work
  - Round nose pliers for forming round loops
  - Needle nose pliers, all purpose
  - Wire clippers needed in jewelry and wire work
- Wax paper for keeping the work surface clean, preventing the clay from sticking to the work surface, and as a baking tray liner
- Wooden skewers for texturing, making holes, and gluing

Liquid polymer clay tool kit

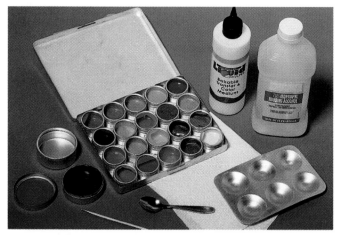

- Translucent Liquid Sculpey, 8 oz. squeeze bottle
- Aluminum box with 20 round 1¼" glass-lidded metal containers, great for storing a range of mixed colors, and makes a great travel case (with the lids taped)
- 2" glass-lidded aluminum containers for storage of larger amounts of tinted liquid clay
- 2¾" glass dishes (not shown) for mixing larger quantities of tinted clay (more than a ½ teaspoon)
- Aluminum palette, each well holds a ½ teaspoon of liquid clay
- Small spoon for scooping mica and other powders
- Dedicated set of teaspoons (not shown) for more precise measuring of materials
- Paper towels for wiping the skewer during color mixing and for general clean up
- Wooden skewer, an indispensable tool for liquid clay color mixing, application, and marbling
- 91% isopropyl alcohol for cleaning up tools and work surface
- Sheet of glass (not shown) at least 5" x 7", used for transfers and for thin sheet baking

Extra tool kit

The following kit outlines a few of the many optional items you will find useful for both solid and liquid polymer clay projects.
- Shape cutters (Ateco) for consistent ovals and circles
- Rubber stamps for texturing
- Friendly clay stamps (Amaco) for concise geometric texture
- Diluent, softener for solid clay or thinner for liquid clay
- T-pin (or pin tool) for etching clay or making holes
- Assorted cutters for cutting shapes
- Leather stamps for making deep detailed impressions
- Metal ruler for straight edges on sheets (metal cannot be damaged when cutting with a blade)
- Cornstarch for a mold release or to prevent cutters and stamps from sticking to the clay
- Shapelets (Polyform Products) templates for creating unique and interesting shapes and creating patterns for larger shapes
- Heat gun for occasional use to set liquid clay before baking
- Extra fine sanding sponge for minimal wet sanding of clay
- Fine grit (400, 600, 800) wet/dry sandpaper (not shown) for more involved sanding
- Flat wooden tool or bone folder for burnishing transfers
- Embossing tool, different sized balls on each end for etching foil or clay
- Pointed wooden stick for smoothing carved molds and for etching patterns onto clay
- Brushes, assorted flat brushes are good for cornstarch, isopropyl alcohol used in transfers, and varnish
- Varnish, Fimo brand (not water based) in gloss and matte finishes are good for sealing mica powders and metallic leaf and for creating a glass-like finish (gloss) on dimensional clay objects
- Odorless brush cleaner, Loew Cornell brand is a good alternative to turpentine

SAFETY REMINDERS
- ■ All work surfaces, tools, and cutters used for polymer clay should not be used for food
- ■ Cutting tools are very sharp—handle with care
- ■ All varnish, brush cleaner, and adhesives should be used carefully in a well-ventilated area
- ■ A dust mask should be worn while using mica, metal and pigment powders, and while wet-sanding
- ■ A heat gun should be handled carefully, as the air is hot and can burn

Basic jewelry findings kit
- Crystal rhinestones for adding sparkle to clay projects
- Eye pins, long (2") and short (⅞"), for connecting beads in necklaces, bracelets, and earrings or as supports in small clay sculptures

- Earring posts, look for titanium or nickel free as hypoallergenic options
- Earring nuts, available in a variety of styles
- Earring hooks (not shown), available in a variety of styles and metal types, look for hypoallergenic types
- Earring clips (not shown), a non-pierced earring option
- Assorted beads for combining with polymer clay elements; available in glass, crystal, bone, wood, stone, and a variety of other materials
- Clear elastic (.8 mm) made for jewelry applications, especially bracelets (not shown)
- Clasps (lobster style shown) for closure and clean finishing on jewelry designs
- Jump rings, gold and silver tone (varied sizes), for quick simple attachment of clasps and for use as connector loops
- Split rings (not shown), a more secure alternative to jump rings
- Pin backs for finishing pins, available in a variety of sizes and qualities
- Glass and stone cabochons for textured embellishment on clay pieces
- Head pins, long (2") and short (⅞"), for earrings and decorative beaded drops
- Beadalon (not shown), a plastic coated multi-strand flexible wire cord for many types and weights of bead stringing
- Crimp beads (not shown), small soft metal beads used to finish the ends on Beadalon, available in a variety of styles and sizes
- Crimp pliers (not shown) for neatly closing the crimp beads
- Memory wire (not shown), pre-shaped steel wire sized for necklaces, bracelets, rings, and anklets, no clasp necessary

- Barrettes (not shown), "made in France" type recommended for longest wear, available in a variety of sizes and styles
- Wire (not shown), available in many gauges for stability, connecting, or decorative elements in jewelry or for armatures

Adhesives kit

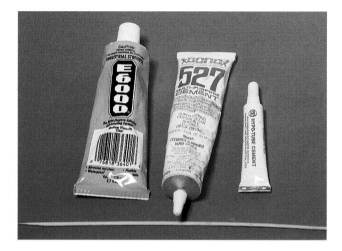

- E-6000 industrial craft glue, all purpose adhesive, important to read instructions for use and safety precautions; do not use to apply foil-backed crystals
- Bond 527 multi-purpose cement for applying foil-backed crystals
- GS Hypo-tube cement, a watchmaker's glue good for gluing knots tied in clear elastic to prevent knot slippage
- Cyanoacrylate glue (not shown) for quick repairs

SAFETY REMINDER

All glues and adhesives should be used with care in a well-ventilated area and with minimal contact to skin. In general, the adhesives should not be baked after application to polymer clay; some adhesives will emit fumes while baking or lose their bonding strength. In some instances, liquid polymer clay can be substituted as a clay adhesive when a piece requires additional baking. An armature can be created for support in order to get full clay adhesion during baking.

FOR MOST OF THE PROJECTS IN THIS BOOK, YOU WILL NEED THE BAKING KIT, THE BASIC TOOL KIT, AND THE LIQUID POLYMER CLAY TOOL KIT. ADDITIONAL TOOLS AND MATERIALS WILL BE LISTED BY PROJECT.

Basic Applications
and Techniques

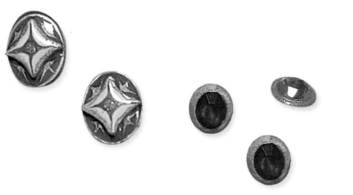

Liquid polymer clay has a wide variety of applications, both practical and creative, that give added versatility and dimension to solid polymer clay. The liquid clay also offers numerous imitative looks not possible with solid polymer clay, and it expands upon the possibilities of applying solid clay to other materials in mixed media applications. As with solid polymer clay, each brand of liquid polymer clay performs differently for each application. There are notations for most applications, explaining the variations in the performance of the two types of clay we tested for this book.

Adhesive Applications

Liquid polymer clay has several valuable adhesive properties when baked. It can be used to bond solid polymer clay elements together, either raw clay to raw or baked clay, or baked clay to baked clay. There are two advantages to using liquid polymer clay instead of glue as a bonding agent with solid polymer clay. First, liquid polymer clay can be baked safely, which is not true for some glues, and second, liquid polymer clay is a similar and compatible material to solid polymer clay, and the two substances will fuse in the baking process for a stronger bond. The liquid clay can also be used to appliqué lightweight or thin solid polymer clay elements to other materials such as wood, papier-mâché, glass, or metal. Several of these mixed media applications are illustrated in the projects in this book.

One exceptional adhesive application for liquid polymer clay is attaching jewelry findings to your solid clay pieces to give your pieces a professional, finished look.

Attaching pin backs

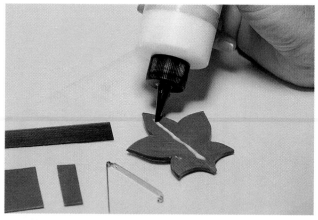

1 • Add clay to back of pin

Squeeze a narrow line of liquid clay the length of your pin back on the back of your baked (and cooled) solid clay pin.

2 • Prepare clay backing

Open the pin back and place it on the back of the pin into the stripe of liquid clay. Make sure the pin opens in the direction that you desire. Roll a small sheet of clay to ¹⁄₁₆" thickness (#4 setting on a pasta machine). Trim to a rectangle ⅜" wide and slightly shorter than the length of the pin back. Spread a thin coat of translucent liquid clay on one side of this rectangle.

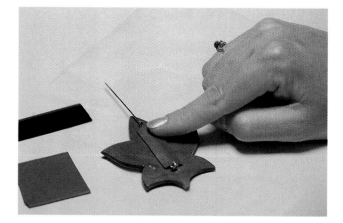

3 • Attach clay backing to pin

Place the side of the rectangle spread with liquid clay face down, centering it over the pin back. Press the rectangle gently onto the clay pin, enclosing the pin back between the baked and unbaked clay. Bake the pin again, back side up, for 15 minutes at 275 degrees (F). Allow to cool.

Attaching earring posts

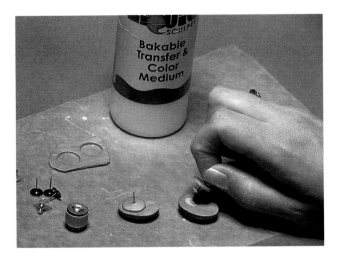

The same method used for attaching pin backs also applies for earring posts.

1. Instead of cutting a rectangular clay strip to cover the pin back, cut two ¹⁄₁₆" thick disks slightly larger than the metal pads on the earring posts.

2. Poke a hole in the center of each disk, spread the disks with liquid clay, and press a disk over the back of each post.

3. Bake the earrings, post sides up, for 15 minutes at 275 degrees (F) and allow them to cool. If you plan to varnish either a pin or a pair of earrings, it is best to attach the pin back or posts and bake before applying the varnish.

Loop reinforcement

Liquid polymer clay can also be used to reinforce loops and wire elements that are embedded in solid clay. Insert the twisted wire end of a loop into unbaked solid clay, place a dot of liquid clay where the loop meets the clay, and bake the clay piece. This will add extra strength to the loop attachment.

Cabochon application

Another adhesive application for the liquid clay includes attaching cabochons (glass, crystal, and stone), tiny glass beads, or glitter to the surface of solid clay or other materials that can be baked.

For cabochons

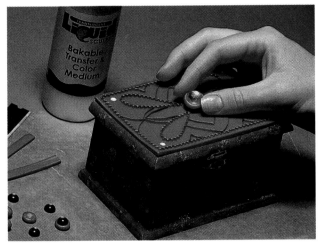

1. Roll a ball of clay the same size as the diameter of the cabochon. Flatten the ball into a disk, apply a dot of liquid clay, and sink the stone into the disk forming a clay bezel around the stone.

2. Place another dot of liquid clay on the project, and set the cabochon with the clay bezel in place.

3. Bake the project, and the stone will be attached.

For glitter or tiny beads

1. Place a ⅛" dot or a very thin line of clay where you would like to place the glitter or tiny beads.

2. Sprinkle the liquid clay with glitter (do not remove the excess), bake, and cool the project.

3. Use a clean dry toothbrush to remove the excess glitter or tiny beads. ***Tip:*** *If you are applying glitter to a solid polymer clay base, make sure the clay base has already been baked and cooled.*

Both the Translucent Liquid Sculpey and the Kato Clear Polyclay Medium performed well for the adhesive applications. The Liquid Sculpey bakes to a matte finish, which is less visible after baking at the edge of the pieces being attached, and the Kato Polyclay Medium bakes to a shiny finish, making the bond more noticeable if the clay is left unvarnished. The Liquid Sculpey is more effective for applying glitter in specific areas, as the Kato Polyclay Medium spreads during baking.

Clay Softener

Stiff polymer clays can be softened in stages by adding a few drops of liquid polymer clay to a ball of clay and kneading it into the solid clay. The liquid clay should be added and mixed in gradually, so as not to soften the clay too much or make it too sticky.

A spackle can be made from solid clay if you continue to add liquid polymer clay and mix it in. Clay spackle is good for filling cracks or repairing previously baked solid clay pieces.

Glazes and Finishes

Glaze for metallic leaf and mica powders

When using metallic leaf or mica powders as a decorative surface treatment on solid polymer clay, the translucent liquid polymer clay can be applied as a glaze that can be baked onto the solid clay as a permanent protective coating. Apply a very thin coat of liquid clay to the leaf or mica, and bake the entire clay piece for 10 minutes at 275 degrees (F).

As a glaze for metallic leaf, the Kato Clear Polyclay Medium is less likely to pull the metallic leaf off the surface of the clay, and it bakes to a very clear satin shine finish. The Translucent Liquid Sculpey bakes to a matte finish with a slightly frosted look. Both liquid clays will smear mica powders slightly. An alternate method for protecting mica powders is to apply a polymer clay varnish (gloss or matte) to the project surface after baking. It is important to protect both metallic leaf and mica powders on a finished project, or they will quickly show signs of wear and rub off of the baked solid clay.

Decoupage

For decoupage, apply a thin layer of translucent liquid clay to the piece being decorated. The item can be made of solid polymer clay or another bake-able material as discussed in the adhesive section. Apply a piece of tissue paper or other type of thin decorative paper, and smooth it over the thin coat of liquid clay, covering the edges of the paper. Add another thin coat of liquid clay, and bake the project for 10 minutes at 275 degrees (F). The two brands of clay work equally well for the decoupage. Once again, the Translucent Liquid Sculpey bakes to a matte finish, and the Kato Clear Polyclay bakes to a shiny finish. Both clays create a water resistant finish on the paper.

Glaze for glass

Softly tinted liquid polymer clay spread in a thin coat and baked can create a sheer glaze on the surface of a glass vessel. Left unvarnished, the glass will appear frosted. When varnished with a gloss finish, the clay leaves only a slight tint of color on the glass. It is best to coat the entire glass object in the liquid clay glaze, instead of coating and baking the glass in stages. If glazed in stages, seams will appear in the liquid clay after baking. Using liquid clay as a glaze for glass is best for decorative and not functional objects, as it is a delicate finish not meant for heavy wear.

Above: Tinted clay has an enameled look and works as a glaze on the metallic leaf.

Right: Decoupage over metal planter and solid polymer clay ornament and brooch.

For the glaze on glass, only the Translucent Liquid Sculpey achieves the desired frosted effect. The Kato Clear Polyclay Medium bakes very clear with a shiny finish. The Kato clay surface has many small bubbles and a tacky feel that noticeably retains fingerprints. The Kato Polyclay medium also drips more, collecting at the bottom rim of the glass, due to its more liquid texture than the Liquid Sculpey.

Transfers

"Transfer" is the term used to describe the application of an image onto polymer clay. Most images are transferred from either a black-and-white or color-toner-based photocopied image or a color laser printed image. The transfer occurs when the paper image is put in contact with the solid or liquid polymer clay, which lifts the toner from the paper when baked. During baking, some artists use liquid polymer clay spread over a sheet of solid polymer clay to aid in the transfer process. A transfer can be made on solid clay before baking, but liquid clay transfers must be baked.

Translucent liquid polymer clay has the advantage over solid clay of creating transfers that are tissue thin and fairly clear. This makes layering of transfer images possible, as well as using the thin image as a window to be set into a frame of clay or other material. The translucent windows are ideal for using on lanterns and votives, as the light will pass through the sheer image. Liquid clay transfers can also be applied to slightly curved surfaces using more translucent clay as an adhesive, which is not possible with a solid clay transfer that is already baked. There are several methods for creating liquid clay transfers. Both the transfer on glass and the transfer from paper methods can be tricky and will require some practice.

Transfer on glass

1. Spread a thin layer of liquid clay on a piece of glass that is larger than your image.

2. Place paper with the image side down over the liquid clay.

3. Smooth the paper into the liquid clay from the center, moving out to the edges and removing air pockets. Allow the image to rest in the liquid clay for five minutes before baking.

4. Bake the paper with the image on the sheet of glass for 15 minutes at 275 degrees (F).

5. Use oven mitts to remove the glass from the oven, set it on a heat resistant surface, and immediately peel the paper with the clay from the glass. While the clay is warm, not hot, peel the paper away from the clay. Make sure the clay does not fold over on itself, as it may stick to itself permanently. A craft knife or a tissue blade can help separate the clay from the paper. Place the clay image on a flat surface to cool. It is now ready to use on your project.

Color can be added to a black and white photocopy image with oil based (not watercolor) pencils such as Prismacolor or Walnut Hollow brands, as well as oil pastels. Freehand drawings drawn with oil-based pencils or pastels will transfer as well, though you may need to test for color change.

Note: *The results will vary with the different types of paper used for photocopies; you may need to test several types. Some papers will not peel easily from the clay. Photocopy images must be copied on a machine that uses toner, as it is the toner that transfers to the clay. The color of the transfer may vary depending on the type of toner.*

Above: Hand-colored thin sheet liquid clay transfers set in polymer clay frames.

Below: Hand mirror and case. On the mirror, the clay fabric is applied over a solid clay base. On the case, the clay fabric has been machine appliquéd to the case fabric.

Transfer from paper

1. Spread a thin even layer of liquid clay directly onto the surface of your image.

2. Place the paper with clay on a flat baking pan and bake for 15 minutes at 275 degrees (F). Use oven mitts to remove it from the oven, and immediately attempt to peel the paper from the clay with the aid of a craft knife.

3. If the paper does not peel away from the clay, place the picture in a bowl of water, and soak for a few minutes. When the picture is saturated, rub the paper off the back of the clay.

Glossy color magazine pictures can be used for this method. The results will vary depending on the quality and type of paper used in the magazine. In general, the results for this method are somewhat inconsistent. It is also difficult to remove the paper completely from the clay. The transfer will look better applied to solid clay than as a sheer window-like transfer.

Other artists have developed an effective method for creating transfers from paper. The liquid clay is spread directly on the paper with the transfer and set with a heat gun. This step is repeated until there are three to four layers of clay (heat set) on the transfer. The clay is then peeled from the transfer and baked at the regular temperature. This method will create a thicker transfer, but it is an effective approach.

With any type of transfer, the image can only be used once. Depending on the application of the transfer to a project, the image may be reversed, which will also reverse any writing on the image. Things that can be used to create transfers include clip art, rubber stamped images, photos, and hand drawn images. All images and designs must be copied or printed with toner before being transferred. If you plan to do production work to sell, it is important that you do not use copyrighted images.

Some artists have used Lasertran silk artist's transfer papers in conjunction with liquid polymer clay on a solid polymer clay base for crisp color transfers. This paper is specifically developed for transfer of images onto mixed media, and it is effective with or without the use of liquid clay.

Both types of liquid polymer clay are effective for transfers. The Translucent Liquid Sculpey transfers are thicker with a somewhat frosted finish, and the Kato Clear Polyclay Medium creates transfers that are quite clear. Both types of clay vary in performance with the types of paper used. The Liquid Sculpey transfers are thicker and have better stability for the window application (sheer, not backed by solid clay), even though it is not completely sheer. The Kato Polyclay Medium transfers are quite clear and very thin, and they are better for transfer layering applications over a solid base.

Applications for Tinted Liquid Polymer Clay

Beyond the basic adhesive and glaze applications, there are many decorative ways to apply tinted liquid clay to enhance your clay or mixed media project.

Painting with clay

Tinted translucent liquid polymer clay can be used to achieve a variety of effects. Liquid clay has a bit more texture than a regular acrylic paint, so layering will create a dimensional effect. There are many ways to paint with clay:

Antiqued clay pendant stippled with several colors of liquid clay.

- Tinted liquid clay can be painted over raw or baked clay to add color. If the clay piece is baked and cooled, another layer of tinted liquid clay can be painted or stippled on for depth.
- Subtle layering of mica-tinted liquid clay colors can create a metallic patinated look. Rubbing a thin layer of dark or light tinted liquid clay over the surface of a dimensional clay piece and then removing part of the liquid layer can produce an antiqued or oxidized effect.
- Liquid clay can be painted or stippled over other materials that can be baked, such as wood or papier-mâché, for a dimensional color base for a project. In its unbaked form, the liquid clay can act as an adhesive for metallic leaf, which can be applied over the unbaked liquid clay and baked onto the surface painted with clay.
- Transfers can be enhanced and given a hand-painted finish with subtle touches of tinted liquid clay over the image.
- Metallic and mica powders in gold tones can be added to the liquid polymer clay to thicken the texture. Applied on the surface or edges of pieces, a rich gilded effect can be achieved.
- Liquid clay tinted with enough pigment or mica powders to thicken the clay can be used to create colored and dimensional scrolls and dots for added texture on the surface of your project.
- Tinted liquid clay can be blended easily over a solid polymer clay, canvas, or wood backing and then baked to create a polymer clay painting.

Painting over a transfer.

Painting, stippling, and gilding with tinted liquid clay on wood.

Impression glazing

Patterns stamped or carved into raw or baked liquid polymer clay can be enhanced by filling the impressions with a tinted contrasting glaze of liquid polymer clay and then baking them. Impression glazing can be divided into three methods, with basically the same result:

Stamp and fill impression glazing consists of texturing solid polymer clay with the traditional method of stamping the clay with rubber or leather stamps or texture sheets, baking the base clay, and then filling the impressions with a glaze of tinted liquid polymer clay and baking again.

The second method of impression glazing utilizes a more abstract form of creating textures, either by using natural materials such as shells, leaves, other assorted natural materials or tools not made for stamping.

The third type of impression glazing uses a molded clay form, either single or double sided, which is baked and glazed in the same way. Nine types of molds will be discussed in the next chapter.

For the painting and the impression glazing applications, both the Translucent Liquid Sculpey and the Kato Clear Polyclay Medium perform well, with the exception of the dimensional effects such as stippling and scrolling. The texture of the Kato Polyclay Medium is too thin to create a crisp, raised scroll pattern, even when heavily tinted with mica powders. This application is better suited to Liquid Sculpey. The Liquid Sculpey bakes to a matte finish, and the Kato Polyclay Medium bakes to a shiny finish.

Above: Stippling, patina, and impression glazing on a solid polymer clay box.

Below: Clay appliqué accented with stippling, dimensional painting, and impression glazing with liquid clay on wood.

Mosaics

Polymer clay is an excellent medium for creating many types of mosaics. Tiles can be made from solid or liquid polymer clay or other bake-able materials. Liquid clay can be used as a tile adhesive and also as a grout. There are numerous ways to make mosaics using a combination of solid and liquid clay:

Tile mosaics

- Baked solid polymer clay tiles can be easily adhered to a raw solid clay base with a thin coating of liquid clay that is then baked, fusing the tiles to the base.
- For a more curved surface and a softer-looking mosaic, raw solid clay tiles can be adhered to a raw or baked solid clay base and then baked.
- Baked or raw solid polymer clay tiles can be adhered to a material other than clay (wood, papier-mâché, glass), once again using liquid clay as the adhesive.

In all three of these applications, tinted liquid clay can be used as the grout once the tiles have been fused to the base with baking. Once the project is cool, the grout is spread over the surface of the mosaic, filling the gaps between the tiles. Excess clay is wiped off the surface of the tiles with a paper towel, and the grout remains in the gaps. The mosaic is baked again and cooled.

Sheet mosaics

As a variation on the more traditional mosaics already described, the thin sheet quality made possible by the liquid clay can be used for some other interesting styles of mosaics.

Flexible sheet mosaics can be created by spreading tinted or translucent liquid polymer clay onto a sheet of glass and laying solid polymer clay tiles on the liquid clay. Bake the whole sheet of mosaics on the glass, and then remove and trim the mosaic with scissors after baking. This sheet mosaic can be applied as a decorative removable cling to a glass container, or it can be adhered to

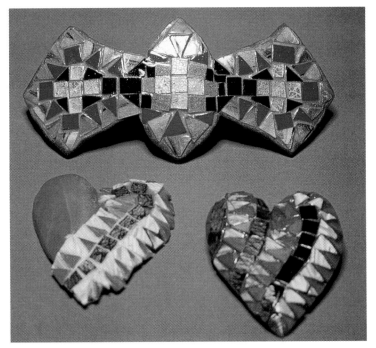

Above: Baked solid clay tiles adhered to a clay base and grouted with a tinted liquid clay.

Below: Baked solid clay tiles adhered to a papier-mâché box and grouted with a tinted liquid clay.

a project using liquid clay as an adhesive (the project must be baked again). The tinted liquid clay tiles can also be baked directly onto glass or another material using liquid clay as the adhesive.

Mica mosaics are a variation of the flexible sheet mosaic made entirely of liquid clay. First, liquid clay tinted with mica flakes, mica powder, or other colorants is spread onto a sheet of glass and baked. Once the cooled sheet is removed from the glass, it is cut into tiles. A thin layer of translucent liquid clay is spread on a sheet of glass, and the baked tinted liquid clay tiles are placed in the clay layer on the glass. The sheet mosaic is baked, cooled, and ready to use.

An inlay effect can be created using tinted thin sheets of liquid clay. First the tinted liquid clay is spread on a sheet of glass, baked, and cooled. Then the sheet can be cut or punched (with scrapbooking scissors or punches) into shaped tiles and placed on a raw base sheet of solid polymer clay coated with liquid clay. To make the inlay, roll the thin tiles into the base sheet of clay with a brayer, and bake the whole piece.

When creating mosaics with both solid and liquid polymer clay, greater detail can be added to the mosaic by giving the tiles some color and texture variations. For added interest on solid clay tiles, consider different surface treatments such as mixed cane veneer, transfers, Skinner blend, metallic leaf, marbling, mokume gane, stamped tiles with mica powder accents, and mica shift veneers. For liquid clay tiles, try adding oil paints, mica powders, mica flakes, and other textural inclusions (see color mixing, page 12).

The Translucent Liquid Sculpey and the Kato Clear Polyclay Medium both work well as adhesives and grout for mosaics. Again, the Liquid Sculpey bakes to a matte finish, and the Kato Polyclay Medium bakes to a shiny finish. For the flexible sheet mosaics with liquid clay tiles, the Kato Clear Polyclay Medium makes very thin mosaics good for removable clings on glass. The Translucent Liquid Sculpey is good for sheet mosaics, but slightly less flexible and not as sheer.

Above: Samples of mica mosaics made from tinted liquid clay.

Below: Surface treatments for solid polymer clay mosaic tiles.

Marbling

Intricate and fluid patterns can be created with liquid clay on the surface of solid clay and other materials. First, spread a thin coat of translucent liquid clay on the surface to be decorated. Next, place a series of fine lines and

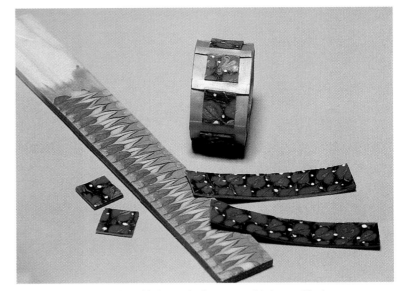

dots of several colors of tinted liquid clay on your project. Drag the pointed tip of a skewer or a pin tool through several of the colors, feathering the colors into patterns. Bake the project to set the marbled surface. Marbling is best enhanced with a coat of clear gloss polymer clay varnish. Applying the same steps on a piece of glass can make thin flexible sheets of marbled liquid clay. Bake and cool the liquid clay. The clay sheet can be peeled from the glass and cut into shapes to apply to a variety of projects.

Only the Translucent Liquid Sculpey works well for the marbling technique. Although the Kato Clear Polyclay Medium bakes very clear and gives marbling a lot of depth in the colors, the consistency is too runny to control easily, and the marbled colors and patterns run together quickly.

Marbling on wood, and marbled mosaic tiles on a solid clay napkin ring.

Marbled earrings.

Glass Effects

Enameling

In jewelry and decorative arts applications, enameling is a method of fusing glass or glasslike materials to a metal base. There are several ways to use liquid polymer clay to create an enamel effect, both with and without a metal or metallic base.

More complex applications of marbling resemble enamel, and they can be achieved by starting with a shaped clay base. Since the entire base will be covered with the marbled pattern, it is not necessary that the base be metal. Several tinted liquid clay colors are placed with a skewer on the base and then marbled with a pin tool (or the pointed tip of the skewer), feathering the colors. Bake the pieces soon after marbling, before the colors can run together.

To make a molded clay base for enameling with clay, use a rubber stamp to make an impression on a sheet of clay (dusted with cornstarch) that is at least ⅛" thick. This will form the mold. Bake and cool the stamped mold. Press a ⅛" thick sheet of cornstarch-dusted solid clay into this mold. This will form your clay base for enamel. Trim the base shape, bake and cool the base, and fill the wells with tinted liquid polymer clay. Bake, cool, and varnish.

Above: Enamel look marbled pin.

Right: Molded clay base with metallic leaf and liquid clay enamel effects.

Below: Cloisonné pin in progress.

Sculpting solid clay snakes into wells and pressing them on a clay base is another technique for creating an enamel look. The base is baked and then the tinted liquid clay is added to the wells. The piece is then baked. A mold can be made from the base before the liquid clay is added, so the pattern can be repeated.

Craft foil also makes a good base for liquid clay enamel. A pattern is embossed on the backside of a sheet of foil. The indented lines are filled with liquid clay and then baked for stability. On the front side, fill the wells created by the embossed lines with tinted liquid polymer clay, and bake again. The foil enamel pieces can either be applied to an object other than clay with an industrial adhesive, or the foil can be backed with solid polymer clay and bent into the desired shape, and baked again.

A metal finding or button can be highlighted with liquid clay and baked to achieve an enamel effect.

With all of these liquid clay enamel techniques, it is important to use a polymer clay gloss varnish to create a glasslike finish and enhance the color and depth of the liquid clay accents.

The Translucent Liquid Sculpey is good for all of the types of clay enameling discussed. The Kato Clear Polyclay Medium works best with the enamel techniques that create wells. Without the use of barriers, the Kato Clear Polyclay Medium is difficult to control, and it will pool at the lowest point on the base.

Cloisonné

Cloisonné is a form of enamel work where the colors of fused glass are separated by metal partitions. This look can also be created in liquid polymer clay. The dividers are best made with folded narrow strips of craft foil or thin strips of metal bent into shapes and pressed into a solid clay backing. As with the clay enamel techniques, it is best to bake the solid clay base with the partitions of foil before adding color. Again, a coat of polymer clay gloss varnish is recommended for a glass-like finish.

Both types of liquid clay can be used for the clay cloisonné look. With the Kato Clear Polyclay Medium, the liquid clay will run out of even the smallest gap in a barrier, and it bakes unevenly. The Liquid Sculpey self-levels and settles more evenly into the wells. Because of the matte finish of the Liquid Sculpey, it must be gloss varnished for the glass-like shine.

Stained glass

As seen in great cathedrals for many centuries, stained glass is a method of combining elements of colored glass connected by lead to make windows or decorative objects. A similar look can be made with polymer clay by creating a lead-colored lattice-work of solid polymer clay, and filling it with translucent liquid polymer clay tinted with the sheer color of oil paints. The clay stained glass panel is then baked. Tinting the liquid clay with mica or other powdered pigments will make the glass-like panels more opaque. It is important to varnish the liquid clay panels in the stained glass with a gloss finish, yet leave the lead-colored clay dividers in the matte finish.

Kato Clear Polyclay Medium offers a clear glass-like look within the clay lead barriers, but it may run slightly between the barriers. The Translucent Liquid Sculpey is not as sheer, but it stays in the barriers and is more level when baked (it does need to be varnished for the glass effect).

Cloisonné style box lid.

Stained glass effects in clay on a vase.

Lampworked beads

Lampwork is a centuries-old technique in bead making, popularized and brought to a high art form by the Italians. The handmade glass beads are decorated with delicate designs of molten glass with the aid of a torch. Fiorato is one of the most recognizable types of lampwork beads. Fiorato beads are most often decorated with scrolling bands of sparkling copper-gold aventurine, and decorated with tiny rosebuds. This miniature art form can now be achieved with the use of liquid polymer clay on a solid clay base bead. With the aid of a skewer and liquid clay heavily tinted and thickened with mica powders, it is possible to make beads resembling the Venetian originals. The liquid clay designs can be set before baking with the help of a heat gun used carefully. The appearance of the Liquid

Sculpey changes from shiny to matte when it is set with the heat gun. Do not scorch the clay. Some artists have executed this technique on base beads fresh from the oven for instantaneous setting of liquid clay placed on a hot bead, but this method does not allow for color blending or changes (unbaked liquid clay on a cool bead can be wiped off if the placement is not desirable), and it is difficult to handle a hot bead. It is important to finish the beads with a gloss varnish for the true shine of glass beads.

Only the Translucent Liquid Sculpey is effective for this technique. The liquid consistency of the Kato Clear Polyclay Medium is too thin for the delicate application involved in this process. Even with heavy mica content, the Kato Polyclay Medium does not reach the paste-like texture needed to form the raised designs.

Clay Sheet Variations

Veneers

Liquid clay sheets baked on glass have numerous applications. As mentioned earlier, baked sheets of tinted clay can be cut up or punched for mosaics. The flexible sheets can also be applied to a clay backing or another material as a veneer. The sheets can be varied depending on the colorants added. Glitter adds a strong sparkle to a veneer sheet when baked on glass.

Clay fabric

Creating clay fabric is a method of infusing (through baking) fabric with liquid clay to create a flexible, water-resistant, non-fraying material for use in polymer clay and mixed media applications. Best results for clay fabric are achieved with a cotton, cotton/polyester blend, or silk fabric, as some synthetics will melt and shrink during baking. Sheer lightweight fabrics allow for greater translucency and flexibility in the clay fabric.

Glossy clay fabric is made by spreading a layer of translucent liquid clay, either tinted or mixed with glitter, on the surface of a sheet of glass. A well-pressed piece of fabric, either of solid color or printed, is laid into the clay. Once the fabric is saturated, it is baked on the piece of glass. When it has been baked, the fabric is peeled away from the glass. It will have the glossy sheen of the surface of the glass.

Patterned fabric can be created through a transfer method. Translucent liquid clay is spread on the paper surface of a photocopy image (copied on a machine with toner). The fabric (solid color or printed) is placed into the clay until saturated. The paper photocopy, clay, and fabric are all baked on a flat tray, and the paper should

Soap dish and liquid clay veneers made with mica powders, oil paints, and glitter.

be peeled away while the fabric is still hot to prevent the paper from sticking to the clay. ***Note:*** *If you have difficulty peeling the fabric away from the image, you can re-heat the fabric with the paper and try to peel again. If some paper remains, soak the fabric in water and rub off the excess paper. Dry the fabric completely before using it on a project. Ease of peeling may be impaired by baking the clay fabric too hot, or using a fabric or paper that is not good for clay transfers. Experiment before attempting larger projects. Check baking temperatures for clay fabric projects.*

Both methods can be embellished and baked again, but the glossy clay may lose some sheen in the second baking. The clay fabric can be hand or machine stitched, wired into dimensional shapes, woven, appliquéd onto regular fabric, punched for lace effects, made into doll clothes, or used as a connector material or flexible hinge in polymer clay projects.

All of the clay fabric projects shown in this book were made with Translucent Liquid Sculpey, with very good results. The Kato Clear Polyclay Medium can be used for both types of the clay fabric listed. The glossy clay made with the Polyclay Medium and glitter has an exceptional sparkle, but it also has a slightly sticky feel due to the high gloss finish.

Projects accented with clay fabric transfers.

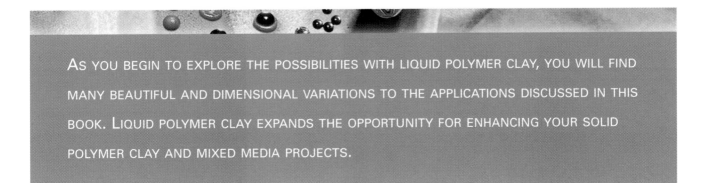

AS YOU BEGIN TO EXPLORE THE POSSIBILITIES WITH LIQUID POLYMER CLAY, YOU WILL FIND MANY BEAUTIFUL AND DIMENSIONAL VARIATIONS TO THE APPLICATIONS DISCUSSED IN THIS BOOK. LIQUID POLYMER CLAY EXPANDS THE OPPORTUNITY FOR ENHANCING YOUR SOLID POLYMER CLAY AND MIXED MEDIA PROJECTS.

Chapter 4

Tips

This chapter presents clay and jewelry tips that can help you with the projects in this book. These hints include methods for molding solid and liquid polymer clay, pattern and transfer designs, jewelry tips, materials preparation for mixed media projects, and measurements.

Making Molds

Stamped mold

A stamped mold is made from an impression of a stamp that allows you to make the reverse image in solid polymer clay.

1. Press an image firmly into a sheet or flattened ball of solid polymer clay at least ¼" thick. The image can be made with rubber, leather, or clay stamps or other tools good for texture.

2. Bake the stamped impression and cool.

3. Dust the baked mold with cornstarch, press a ball or sheet of solid unbaked clay into the mold, and remove the molded pattern. Embellish and bake.

Carved transfer mold

This is a type of mold made by carving in solid unbaked clay by using a transfer to create a pattern. The method of applying the transfer to solid clay with rubbing alcohol and burnishing is attributed to artist Gwen Gibson.

1. Select a simple black and white image that has been photocopied on a machine that uses toner. Gently burnish the paper with the image onto the clay using a flat-edged wooden tool or bone folder.

2. Using a flat brush, saturate the backside of the transfer image with isopropyl alcohol. Allow the paper to dry. Burnish the paper once again. Brush on a second coat of alcohol, saturating the paper.

3. While still saturated, gently peel back a corner of the paper to check that the image has transferred. If not, allow the paper to dry, burnish again, and saturate a third time. When the image has clearly transferred to the clay, peel away the paper. If the toner is slightly sticky, dust the image with a light coating of cornstarch.

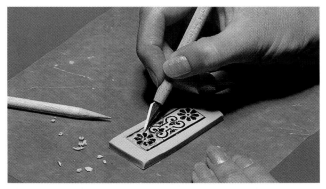

4. With a beveled edge metal tool or a craft knife, carve away the parts of the image that do not have ink. Remove the excess clay, and pat down the carved area with a pointed wooden tool. After the entire pattern has been carved, trim the edges of the carved image with a tissue blade. Bake the carved mold and cool. The mold is ready to use.

Carved mold

A carved mold can be made without a transfer, using a ¼" thick (or thicker) sheet of baked solid polymer clay. The image is cut out with a linoleum cutting tool, wood carving tools, or a craft knife.

Reverse mold

You can create a reverse mold by making a mold from your stamped or carved mold. This will allow you to make a polymer clay piece that duplicates the original image.

1. Make a ¼" thick sheet of solid polymer clay and cut it slightly larger than the mold you are using (it can be a stamped or carved mold).

2. Brush the mold with cornstarch, and press the sheet of unbaked clay into the mold using your thumbs.

3. Remove the molded sheet, trim and bake. This is now your reverse mold.

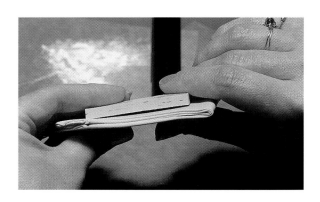

Double sided mold

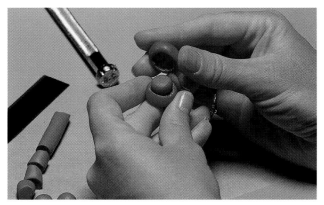

1. Roll two balls of solid polymer clay the same diameter as the width of your stamp. Flatten the balls to form disks. Dust the flattened surfaces of the balls with cornstarch. Using a rubber stamp, leather stamp, or a textured button, make a fairly deep impression on one of the flattened balls. Make the same impression on the second flattened ball. Bake the stamped clay impressions, and allow the molds to cool.

2. Dust both molds with cornstarch. Roll a ball slightly smaller in diameter than the width of the first impression mold. Set the ball of clay into the first mold. Align the second mold over the first, sandwiching the ball of unbaked clay. Gently press the molds together. Do not squeeze the clay out beyond the edges of the impressions.

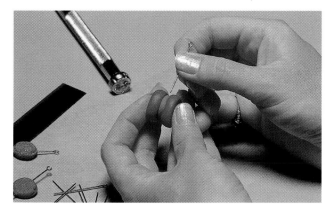

3. Before removing the clay from the molds, pierce the bead through the center with an eye pin to form the bead hole. Remove the bead from the molds, and bake it with the eye pin in the bead. Glaze or embellish the bead as desired.

Multiple-element mold

For creating larger molds best used for solid polymer clay veneers or panels, you can make a textural multiple-element mold. To do this, combine the elements of smaller stamps to form a larger pattern. This new stamped image is then baked and cooled, and it can be used in the same way as the molds described previously.

Sculpted mold

A mold can be hand formed for more abstract designs or to make backings with deep wells for the liquid clay enamel and cloisonné techniques.

1. Roll a sheet of clay to a ⅛" thickness, and cut it into the desired backing shape.

2. Roll a second sheet of clay to a ⅛" thickness. Cut ¹⁄₁₆" wide strips from the sheet. Use these strips to form shapes or closed wells on the backing sheet. Press the shapes gently onto the backing. Bake and cool the clay.

3. Make a mold of the sculpted shape (refer to reverse mold, page 39). Bake and cool the mold. Pieces made from this mold will have the enclosed wells of the original sculpted shape, and can be filled with tinted liquid polymer clay for an enamel or cloisonné effect.

Flexible molds for polymer clay are made from real leaves.

Purchased molds

Both Polyform and Amaco offer a good selection of rubber molds, excellent for molding solid polymer clay into shapes ranging from doll parts to animals, flowers, and decorative edges and medallions. Molded clay items can be easily applied to clay or other materials with liquid clay as an adhesive and tinted liquid clay as an antiquing glaze.

For all of the molds described previously for solid polymer clay, the molds should be coated with a release agent or the polymer clay may stick in the mold. Cornstarch or a talc-free baby powder works well, and it will brush off the clay after baking.

Molding liquid polymer clay

Liquid polymer clay lends itself to being molded for thin sheets and very delicate elements that can be applied to clay or other projects. The difficulty with molding the liquid clay is that it must be baked in the mold, so it is important that the mold be resistant to the baking temperature. Silicone based molds are the best choice.

Leather stamps, objects, and natural materials such as leaves and shells make the best impressions for molds. If you plan to make a mold from an object, you should brush the surface of the molding material with a coat of cornstarch before making the impression. Once the molding material has cured completely, you can pour or brush your tinted liquid clay into the mold.

Allow the mold with the liquid clay to set for 30 minutes to allow air bubbles in the clay to rise to the surface. Pop the bubbles with a pin, and bake the mold with the clay. Remove the mold with the baked liquid clay from the oven, allow it to cool, and the flexible mold will allow for easy removal of the liquid clay element. Results may vary based on tinting material used for the liquid clay. Using a cabochon mold, sparkling gems in single or layered colors can be formed with liquid polymer clay tinted with glitter and mica powder and finished with a coat of varnish. Tests have been made with a new material called FlexiClay with good results. Because of the incredibly fine detail made possible by the Flexi-clay, paper-thin molds of leaves can be made. At the time of publication, FlexiClay was not yet available for purchase.

Note: *In some cases, liquid polymer clay can be molded in a solid polymer clay mold. The pre-baked solid clay mold must be well powdered with cornstarch before adding the liquid clay, and once baked, the liquid clay must be removed from the mold while it is still hot. Results with this approach can be mixed.*

Pattern Design

Creating composite transfers

There are many different ways transfers can be used to enhance your polymer clay projects. Images can be reduced or enlarged or layered in order to fit the size and style of your project. As mentioned before, images can be created with clip art, rubber stamps, photos or freehand drawing, or even a combination of all of these approaches.

1. Determine the size of the transfer needed for your project. If you use clip art or stamps, make a photocopy of the image, reducing or enlarging the image to fit the object. If necessary, make multiple copies of the image in the appropriate size, and trim the images with scissors. Also, a combination of different images can be placed on one sheet to form a composite transfer.

2. Lay the cut out images on a plain white sheet of paper, overlapping and matching the pattern carefully, and use a clear tape or stick glue to attach them to the white sheet. Allow at least ¼" of space around the outer edge of the transfer. This will make the transfer process easier.

3. Photocopy the composite image. This will be your transfer sheet.

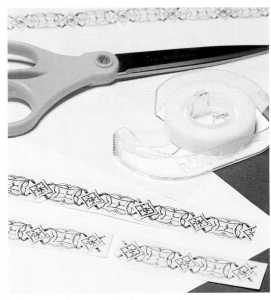
Photocopy clip art or other images to form a composite transfer.

Layered transfers

Several thin sheet transfers made with liquid polymer clay can be layered to create an image with depth on a flat or curved surface. The images are adhered with a thin layer of translucent liquid clay between each clay transfer, and then they are baked onto a base. For more information regarding making transfers, refer to Transfers, page 25.

Note: *Paper selection is very important for transfers, and it may require some trial and error. A paper with too much fiber on the surface may not peel well; a smooth finish is better. Photocopies must be made on either a black and white or color copier with toner, as it is the toner that transfers to the polymer clay. The tinting medium, baking temperature, and diluent can also affect the ease of peeling in liquid clay transfers.*

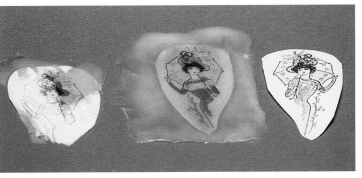
A partially and fully peeled transfer image. The difference was in the paper.

Project patterns using Shapelets

Polyform's Shapelets, designed by Barbara McGuire, make good tools for designing bases for clay projects. Shapelets are thin, translucent, plastic shapes that can be traced onto paper or directly onto polymer clay. They can be used as single shapes, or they can be combined by sketching them on paper to make more complex shapes, depending on the size and style of the project. If necessary, the newly created shapes can be reduced or enlarged on the photocopier. Shapelets were used to create the impression glazing barrette (page 66) and the cloisonné pin (page 121).

Shapelets can be traced onto paper or directly onto polymer clay.

Jewelry Tips

Many polymer clay artists create beads and sculptural elements to incorporate into jewelry. These hints for basic jewelry construction are drawn from the many years of the authors' experiences in production jewelry making. The tips include using crimp beads with pliable wire cord, adding a clasp, memory wire, and using head pins and eye pins.

Crimp beads

One of the most effective methods for stringing beads of all sizes and weights is to use crimp beads in combination with a flexible plastic-coated multi-strand steel cord. One of the popular brands is Beadalon, and it comes in a variety of diameters—sizes .015" (.38 mm) and .018" (.46 mm) being the most versatile. A crimp bead is a small, soft, metal bead or tube that is approximately 2 mm in diameter and 1 to 2 mm wide. Some are smooth and some textured. Larger sizes of crimp beads are available for thicker and multiple strands of the wire cord. It is a good idea to purchase a pair of crimp pliers if you plan to do a lot of stringing, as these pliers will give the crimp beads a cleaner finish.

1. Slide a crimp bead on the end of the Beadalon cord. Loop the end of the cable through a jump ring or split ring and then back through the crimp bead.

2. Use the inner groove of the crimp pliers to press an indentation into the crimp bead.

3. Use the outer circular groove of the crimp pliers to fold the crimp bead in half and secure it over the cable.

4. Trim the excess cable extending beyond the crimp bead.

5. When all the beads are strung on the cable, add a crimp bead and split ring as you did on the beginning of the necklace, trimming the excess cable.

Note: *Needle nose pliers can be used to flatten a crimp bead securely over the two strands of cable, but sometimes this will leave a sharp edge that can be felt while wearing a necklace or bracelet.*

Adding a clasp

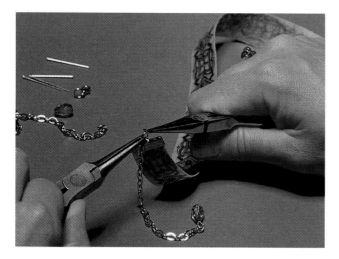

There are many types of clasps available; your choice is based on personal preference. The projects in this book use lobster claw clasps, named after their shape. In most cases, a clasp will require a loop to attach it to the beaded strand and a larger loop to hook into.

There are two basic types of loops for attaching clasps. The first, and easiest to use, is a jump ring. A jump ring is a loop with an opening on one side. A jump ring can be carefully opened and shut by using two pairs of needle nose pliers or a pair of pliers and your fingers to open the small gap in the loop. To do this, move the ends of the loop in opposite directions from each other, without altering the curve of the loop. After the loop is in place, move the ends of the jump ring flush with each other, so there is no gap for the cord to slip out. If you bend the shape of the loop by pulling the ends away from each other at the gap, it is difficult to reshape the loop and close the gap completely.

A split ring is a double loop, so the ends cannot gap. These are more secure but also more difficult to attach. Split rings are good for the end loops on necklaces and bracelets, where the flexible wire cable can be pulled through and crimped onto the loop. To attach the split ring to the clasp, lift one end of the split ring away from the rest of the loop just enough to slide the clasp on. Slide the clasp around until it is all the way on the split ring. The process is much like attaching a key to a key chain ring.

When finishing a necklace or bracelet, crimp a wire cord loop around a medium sized jump or split ring on one end of the beaded strand, and crimp a wire cord loop around the smaller jump or split ring that runs through the connecting loop on the clasp on the opposite end. The projects in this book are completed with jump rings.

Memory wire

Memory wire is a type of 22 gauge (.025") tempered steel wire that maintains its shape. Memory wire can be purchased in several different sizes appropriate for making necklaces, bracelets, and rings. The wire comes in a continuous coil that must be cut to a specific length, which makes it especially good for beading multi-strand pieces. The advantage of using memory wire is that it does not require a clasp for closure, as the wire retains its shape.

There are three ways to finish the ends of the memory wire.

The first option is to form a small loop at the end of the wire with a pair of round nose pliers. The wire is very stiff, and it will be difficult to shape. Make sure there is not a sharp end sticking out of the loop that may be irritating when the finished item is worn. Decorative drops can be added to the end loops later.

For the second option, you can bend the first end of the wire into a small hook shape and then string the beads for the project. Embed each end with a hook into a ball of clay. Bake the entire piece and let it cool. Make sure to combine clay beads with other beads and elements made of heat resistant materials that can withstand baking. The hooks in the wire act as anchors to secure the polymer clay balls on the wire ends, which will prevent the rest of the beads from sliding off the wire.

For the third method of finishing ends on memory wire, there are special small metal ball ends with half drilled holes that can be slid onto the cut end of the wire and secured with a dot of glue that is effective for metal adhesion. This type of finish has moderate durability over time, the balls may detach eventually. When adding beads, it is difficult to glue the end ball in place on the second end without the beads falling off.

It is a good idea to use a pair of heavy-duty wire clippers to cut memory wire, as the very tough steel wire will mar the edges of finer wire clippers. Memory wire is good for stringing most types of beads, but it may be too thick to accommodate smaller seed beads.

Using head pins for drops

Head pins can be used for decorative drops or to make drops for earrings. A head pin is a piece of wire with a flat disk or head attached to the end. Plated brass head pins come in assorted lengths (⅞" to 4") and diameters (thin .025", standard .028", and thick .032"). Standard thickness headpins are a good weight for most glass beads, but they may be too thick for seed beads and semi-precious stone beads or pearls. Sterling and gold-filled wires are usually thinner but not as readily available in assorted lengths.

1. To form a simple drop, slide a bead onto the head pin, so the head is flush with the bottom of the bead. There should be at least ⅜" of the head pin wire sticking out of the top of the bead. Where the wire exits the bead, use your round nose pliers to bend the wire at a 90 degree angle horizontally.

2. Next bend the wire back in the opposite direction, forming a ⅛" loop.

3. Trim the excess wire with wire clippers.

4. Hook the loop on the drop to the connecting loop on the project or to an earring hook. Close the loop on the drop with your pliers.

If you are using a bead with a hole larger than the head of the pin, you may need to add a bead cap or a bead with a smaller hole below the large hole bead to keep it from sliding off the head pin.

Connecting beads with eye pins

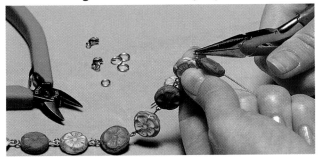

Like head pins, eye pins come in a variety of lengths and diameters. An eye pin is a piece of wire with a preformed loop at one end. You should select a length that is only ⅜" to ½" longer than the diameter of the bead you will be placing on the eye pin to avoid excess waste in the wire you trim off.

1. Slide a bead onto the eye pin, placing one side of the bead flush with the loop on the end of the eye pin. There should be at least ⅜" of the eye pin wire sticking out of the other side of the bead. Where the wire exits the bead, use your round nose pliers to bend the wire at a 90 degree angle.

2. Bend the wire back in the opposite direction, forming a ⅛" loop.

3. Trim the excess wire with wire clippers.

4. Hook the open loop through the closed loop of another eye pin. Attach the next bead in the same fashion as the first, forming a loop at the other end of the second eye pin.

5. Repeat this process for all the beads you wish to connect.

The eye pin loops will form a textural chain effect between the connected beads, and they will give the piece flexibility.

Materials Preparation

Wood preparation

When using wood for a base on liquid clay projects, it is a good idea to remove some of the moisture before applying the clay. This cuts down on the bubbling of the clay on the surface. Wood may crack slightly as it dries; consider this an added texture to your project.

1. Preheat the oven as you would for baking polymer clay, at 265 degrees (F).

2. Place the wood item on a baking tray, and bake for 20 minutes.

3. Once cooled, use a medium grit sandpaper to rub the surface of the wood. Sanding the surface will help the clay adhere better to the wood.

4. With a soft cloth or paper towel, remove the excess residue from the surface of the wood. It is now ready for liquid clay application.

Note: *Since wood is flammable, it is important to closely supervise the baking process for any projects with a wood base. The same caution applies to projects with a papier-mâché base.*

Glass and metal preparation

If you are applying liquid polymer clay to a glass or metal base as a permanent glaze, the base should be cleaned first with a paper towel dampened with isopropyl alcohol. This will help remove any oils, dust, and other residue and aid in better clay adhesion.

Note: *Metal and glass heat up very quickly during the baking process. Carefully supervise the clay to keep it from getting overheated on these surfaces. Glass needs to be cooled slowly to prevent cracking. Metal and glass need to be cooled completely after baking before another layer of liquid clay is added, or the clay will start to cure immediately upon application.*

Solid Polymer Clay Sheets

For several of the projects in this book, you will be using sheets of clay thicker than standard pasta machine settings. To best achieve a sheet with a smooth uniform thickness, choose a setting on the pasta machine half the thickness you desire. Roll a sheet of conditioned solid polymer clay at this thickness, cut the sheet in half with your tissue blade, and layer the two sheets together. Roll from the center of the sheet out to the edges with a brayer. This will remove the air pockets and help the sheets stick together. If you use sheets of two different colors, you can continue to cut up the sheets and layer them; this is an easy way to make a striped loaf. Thin slices can be sliced off the side of the striped loaf with a tissue blade and placed on a backing sheet of clay to make a striped veneer.

Measurements

The following is a standardized list for measurements used in this book.

Quantities of clay

In reference to solid polymer clay (Premo was used in this book):

One block = 2 ounces = 56 grams of clay
One brick = 1 pound = 454 grams of clay

Pasta machine settings

For Atlas pasta machine settings (thickness of each sheet, according to the machine used in this book):

#1 setting: ⅛" (slightly less) or 2.9 mm
#2 setting: ³⁄₃₂" or 2.4 mm
#3 setting: ⁵⁄₆₄" or 2.0 mm
#4 setting: ¹⁄₁₆" or 1.6 mm
#5 setting: ³⁄₆₄" (slightly more) or 1.2 mm
#6 setting: ¹⁄₃₂" or .8 mm
#7 setting: ¹⁄₆₄" (slightly more) or .5 mm

Baking temperature conversion

265 degrees Fahrenheit = 130 degrees Celsius
275 degrees Fahrenheit = 135 degrees Celsius

Bead and cabochon measurements

For cabochons and beads, measurements are often shown in millimeters. Some popular sizes for beads are:

3 mm = .118 inches
4 mm = .157 inches
5 mm = .196 inches
6 mm = .236 inches
8 mm = .314 inches
10 mm = .393 inches
12 mm = .472 inches
14 mm = .551 inches

Wire gauges

Wire is measured by gauge, as marked on the spool. A larger gauge number indicates a smaller diameter or thinner wire. For example, an 18 gauge wire has an approximate diameter of 1.0 mm, and a 26 gauge wire has a diameter of .4 mm.

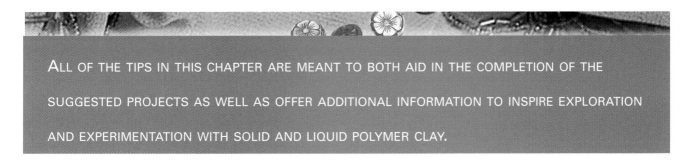

ALL OF THE TIPS IN THIS CHAPTER ARE MEANT TO BOTH AID IN THE COMPLETION OF THE SUGGESTED PROJECTS AS WELL AS OFFER ADDITIONAL INFORMATION TO INSPIRE EXPLORATION AND EXPERIMENTATION WITH SOLID AND LIQUID POLYMER CLAY.

Chapter 5

Images and Transfers

Creating Art

Cameos are an excellent example of the evolution of imagery. Originated by the Egyptians in 300 B.C., cameos of the Greeks and Romans bore images of gods and goddesses. Early cameos were carved from gems, lava, or stone and were popular with both men and women. Cameos carved out of shell became more popular at the beginning of the nineteenth century, as did the female profile associated with cameos today.[6]

Art has been described as an "aesthetic object," that which concerns the beautiful and is conditional to the varied cultural influences of our multi-faceted world. Art can be a concrete demonstration of the imagination or an interpretation of the daily activities of any given culture.[1] Art is created as an adornment to our environment and as a form of communication. Every artist attempts to interpret her or his world in her or his own special style. Inspiration for any art can come from a multitude of different sources. An artist can be influenced by many visual ingredients, some of them historical in source and oftentimes completely unrelated to the object being created.

In each of these project chapters there is a brief historical background of the technique or idea that has inspired each type of liquid polymer clay application. Also included are inspirational photographs of a variety of objects that demonstrate that technique. the photographs also offer additional inspiration for the application of that technique to a new medium such as polymer clay. It is important for all artists to learn techniques, but then to use their own unique creativity to move forward with their work and make it their own. At the conclusion of each project chapter there is a gallery of ideas presenting variations of the techniques covered in the chapter.

Imagery in Art

Imagery is the means of creating a style or effect through the physical representation of a person, animal, object, or pattern.[2] The earliest known examples of imagery in art are cave drawings from the late Paleolithic period. These early images of herds of animals were probably drawn as part of a magic ritual to conjure up greater numbers of bison or deer for the hunt as these animals became scarcer in the receding Ice Age.[3] These ancient illustrations and the imagery that follows throughout history represent the telling of a story, a means of communication. The primitive art from 15,000 years ago "spoke" of fertility magic through sculpture and masks. In Egypt and Mesopotamia, images shifted away from the depiction of nature toward the illustration of humans and their daily lives. The Egyptians specialized in portraiture of their rulers and the celebration of life in death.[4]

Egyptian portraiture was revived later by the early Romans and again by the Italians who painted on glass. Portraiture over the centuries has allowed artists to paint the many facets of human characteristics and tell stories of the human condition.[5] In the continuation of history, imagery has been a means of visualization of stories and religious icons. Religion has prompted the exploration and refinement of many art forms. Religious organizations sought out and supported artists and craftsmen that specialized in varied areas such as architecture, sculpture, mosaics, stained glass, and word carving. People are drawn to imagery in art because it evokes emotions, makes cultural statements, and reveals a story. Applying images to your artwork can give your pieces an antique or exotic feel, transporting the viewer to another place or time.

Over time each culture develops a certain artistic style that becomes very recognizable. Specific images and patterns can be sourced as being Japanese, Italian, African, or from a myriad of other cultures. Using various cultural images gives an artist's work a certain dimension and evokes a response or feeling associated with that culture.

Imagery on Polymer Clay

The artist can embellish and enhance her or his works through the use of historic images and patterns. One of the most popular ways of presenting imagery on polymer clay is through the use of transfers. Images can come from a variety of sources including rubber stamps, historical or contemporary clip art, or drawings. Liquid polymer clay can be used to make a number of different types of transfers.

Liquid clay allows us to make a thin sheer transfer using glass. This allows for the addition of sheer pictorial elements into polymer clay work. The first two projects in this chapter present ways of incorporating transparent sheets into solid polymer clay frames. The first project, reminiscent of a decorative painted glass portrait, uses a hand-colored transfer in an ornamental frame. The second project, the candle lamp, uses a simple black and white transfer to create the look inspired by the magnificent windows of Notre Dame in Paris.

The third and fourth projects in this chapter explore clay fabric. On both pieces, the clay fabric has been enhanced with the use of transfers to give it a more interesting appeal. For the choker, the transfer has been hand colored and the design further enhanced with glass stones. The transfer on the clay fabric purse gives the feel of an all-over pattern on printed fabric. An enormous number of historical and cultural images are available to the artist. It is important to find those images that suit your style and personality.

Transfer Cameo Pendant

MATERIALS&TOOLS

- ½ block gold Premo
- Cameo pendant transfer image (page 136)
- 18" piece of gold tone chain
- 1 lobster claw clasp, 11 mm
- 3 gold tone jump rings, ¼"
- 3 gold tone head pins, 1"
- 1 fresh water pearl, 6mm
- 1 fresh water pearl, 8mm
- 6" fabric trim, ¼" wide
- Basic tool kit (refer to page 17)
- Liquid polymer clay tool kit (refer to page 18)
- Baking kit (refer to page 17)

- 2 oval cookie cutters, 1¼" x 1", 1⅞" x 1⅝"
- Oil-based color pencils: metallic green (umbrella), pumpkin orange (flowers), blush pink (skin), Tuscan red (dress), terra cotta (hat), yellow ochre (trim/feathers)
- Optional: Fine wire, 28 gauge or thinner

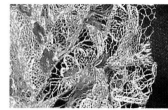

1 • Color the transfer image

Make a copy of the cameo pendant transfer image on a copier that uses toner. Color the image with colored pencils, as desired.

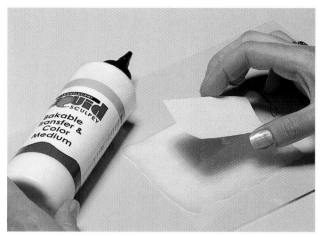

2 • Make the clay transfer

Refer to Transfer on glass (page 25). Spread a thin layer of liquid polymer clay on a sheet of glass slightly larger than the transfer sheet. Place the transfer image into the clay, colored side down. Let the transfer rest for 5 to 10 minutes, and then bake the transfer on glass for 15 minutes at 275 degrees (F).

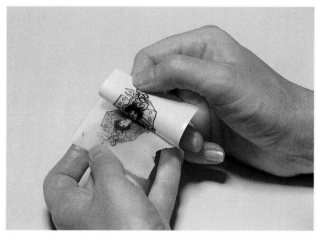

3 • Peel the paper from the transfer

Use oven mitts to remove the transfer on glass from the oven. Immediately peel the paper with the clay from the glass. While the clay is warm, not hot, peel the paper away from the clay. Cool the clay transfer on a flat surface.

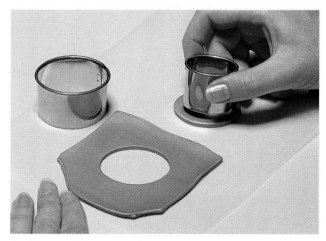

4 • Prepare the cameo frame

Condition the gold Premo and roll it out to a ⅛" thickness (#1 setting). Cut out the picture "frame" using two oval cookie cutters, two sizes apart. Cut out the larger oval first, and then center the smaller oval inside. Remove the center cutout. Smooth the edges of the clay frame with your fingertip.

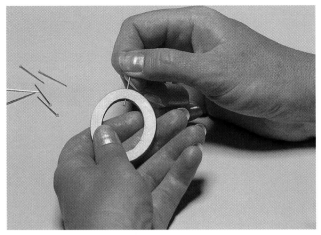

5 • Insert the head pins
Carefully push one headpin through the top of the oval frame from the inside edge to the outside edge. Repeat at the bottom of the frame.

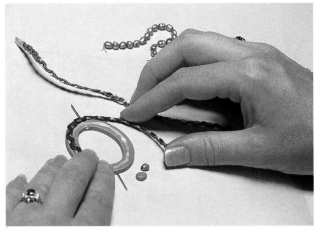

6 • Attach the trim
Cut 3" of fabric trim. To avoid fraying, ends can be wrapped in fine wire. On a piece of wax paper, saturate the trim with liquid clay and remove the excess clay. Squeeze a line of liquid clay around the front of the frame. Lay the trim around the face of the frame, covering the place where the ends meet with a ³⁄₁₆" ball of gold clay. Squeeze a tiny dot of liquid clay on the gold ball and press in the 6 mm fresh water pearl. Bake the frame on a piece of glass for 15 minutes at 275 degrees (F).

7 • Attach the transfer to the frame
Lay the frame over the transfer picture, mark the oval with a pencil, and cut it out. Spread liquid clay onto the backside of the frame. Center the opening over the transfer picture, and place the frame onto the transfer. Bake for 10 minutes at 275 degrees (F).

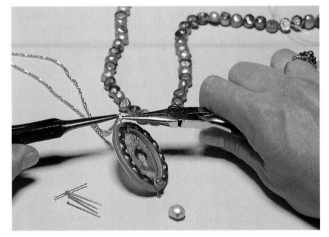

8 • Finish the necklace
Make an 8 mm pearl drop for the pendant (refer to using head pins for drops, page 43). Using pliers, turn over the head pins at the top and bottom of the pendant to form loops, clip off the excess wire, and close the loops. Attach the pearl drop to the loop at the bottom of the pendant. Attach the pendant to the center of the chain using a jump ring. Attach the clasp to the chain (refer to Adding a clasp, page 42).

Transfer Window Candle Lamp

MATERIALS & TOOLS

- 4 blocks purple Premo
- Pattern for candle lamp (page 136)
- Transfer for candle lamp (page 136)
- 12" gold tone wire, 20 gauge
- 4 gold tone head pins, 1"
- 4 purple glass oval beads, 7 mm x 12 mm
- Basic tool kit (refer to page 17)
- Liquid polymer clay tool kit (refer to page 18)
- Baking kit (refer to page 17)
- 1 round cookie cutter, 2¼" diameter

- Plastic texture sheet, cut to fit through pasta machine
- Pint or quart size milk carton, cleaned and dried
- Pearl Ex Aztec gold mica pigment powder
- Soft brush, ½"
- Aluminum foil
- Small votive candle in a metal or glass holder

1 • Texture the clay sheets

Condition one block of purple clay. Roll out a ⅛" thick sheet (#1 setting). Using the soft brush, powder the plastic texture sheet with Aztec gold mica powder (it does not have to be an even coat). Lay the purple clay sheet over the powdered side of the plastic texture sheet and roll them together through the pasta machine on the thickest setting (#1 setting). Repeat this step with the other three blocks of clay, resulting in four textured sheets.

2 • Cut out the lamp panels

Using the candle lamp pattern, cut out the four sides, one from each piece of textured clay. Use the round cookie cutter to cut out a circular window from each piece, centered horizontally on the pattern and ½" above the base. Bake at 275 degrees (F) for 20 minutes. Cool the panels flat.

3 • Make the transfers

On a copy machine that uses toner, make four copies of the transfer pattern and cut them out, leaving ½" of blank paper around each design. Spread a thin layer of liquid polymer clay on a sheet of glass slightly larger than the transfer sheet (refer to Transfer on glass, page 25). Place the transfer into the clay, toner side down. Let the transfer rest for 5 to 10 minutes, and then bake it on the glass for 15 minutes at 275 degrees (F). Use oven mitts to remove the transfer on glass from the oven. Immediately peel the paper with the clay from the glass. While the clay is warm, not hot, peel the paper away from the clay. Cool the clay transfer on a flat surface. Make four transfers using this method. Trim all four transfers into round shapes ⅛" to ¼" larger than the round holes cut in the sides of the lamp panels.

4 • Attach the transfers to the panels

Squeeze a line of liquid clay around the window on the non-textured back of a lamp panel. Spread the clay flat with your finger. Center a transfer over the hole (you can choose if you would like the shiny or the matte side to face out), and place the transfer onto the liquid clay. Bake the panel with the textured side up on a sheet of glass for 10 minutes at 275 degrees (F). Cool the panel and transfer flat. Repeat for all four sides.

5 • Attach the panels to each other

Using the excess purple solid polymer clay, roll a clay ribbon ⅜" x 11½" that is 1/16" thick (#4 setting). Cut off the top of the milk carton, leaving 4" sides on the remaining bottom section. Cover the bottom section with aluminum foil. Wrap the clay ribbon all the way around the very bottom of the carton, overlapping the ends slightly and trimming off the excess. Cover the clay ribbon with a thin layer of liquid clay. Carefully place each side of the candle lamp against each side of the clay-ribbon-wrapped carton, making sure that all the sides are touching the clay ribbon. Wrap a piece of foil around the entire lamp to keep the sides in place during baking. Bake at 275 degrees (F) for 15 minutes.

6 • Attach corner twists

Roll purple clay into two ³⁄₁₆" x 14" snakes. Twist the two snakes together to form a twisted snake, and cut off four 3¼" pieces. Squeeze a line of liquid clay in the corner of the lamp and apply a twist onto it. Repeat for the other three corners. Trim the twisted snakes at the top and bottom of the panels. Bake for 15 minutes at 275 degrees (F).

7 • Attach the base to the candle lamp

Roll out a ⅛" sheet of clay (#1 setting) slightly larger than 3" x 3". Place the candle lamp over the sheet, and cut out a base following the sides of the lamp. Pick up the lamp, apply a line of liquid clay to the base where the sides meet it, and place the lamp back down on the base. Bake for 15 minutes at 275 degrees (F).

8 • Make the wire spirals

Cut four pieces of gold tone wire 2½" long. With round nosed pliers, bend each piece into a flat spiral with a ½" straight end.

9 • Attach the spirals

Roll out a ³⁄₃₂" thick sheet (#2 setting) of purple clay that is ½" x 1½". Cut four isosceles triangles with ¾" sides and a ½" base. Coat one side of each triangle with liquid clay. Place the straight end of a wire spiral against the coated side of a triangle with the curved part of the spiral extending over the center point of the isosceles triangle. Press the clay coated triangle against the inside of a peak of one of the panels of the lamp. The wire should be sandwiched between the clay triangle and the inside of the lamp. Repeat for the other three spirals. Bake at 275 degrees (F) for 15 minutes. ***Note:*** *If the lamp is now too tall for your oven, you may need to attach only one or two spirals at a time and bake the lamp propped to the side.*

10 • Attach the beaded drops

Remove the carton from the lamp. Place each purple bead on a gold tone headpin, and form a loop with the round nose pliers (refer to using head pins for drops, page 43). Attach a drop to each spiral. Place a small votive candle (in a metal or glass holder) in the center of the lamp.

Clay Fabric Choker

MATERIALS & TOOLS

- Any color unbaked solid polymer clay, ¼" ball
- Light green fabric strip, sheer cotton or sheer cotton/polyester blend, well pressed, 3" x 15" or larger
- Transfer for clay fabric choker (page 136)
- Gold tone chain with round links, 4½" to 5"
- 2 gold tone choker ends, ¾" wide
- 1 small lobster claw clasp
- 2 gold tone loops, ¼" diameter
- 1 gold tone head pin, ¾"
- 1 small glass bead

- 9 lavender glass or crystal rhinestones with flat backs, ⅛"
- Basic tool kit (refer to page 17)
- Liquid polymer clay tool kit (refer to page 18)
- Baking kit (refer to page 17)
- Oil-based color pencils: violet, imperial violet, yellow ochre, green
- Ruler
- Optional: E-6000 industrial craft glue
- Optional: Bond 527 multi-purpose cement

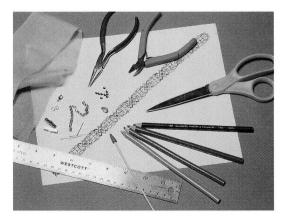

1 • Color the transfer image

Make a copy of the transfer image on a copier that uses toner. Prepare the image for transfer (refer to Creating composite transfers, page 41). Piece together an image that measures 12" x ¾". Color the image with four colors of pencils, as desired.

2 • Clay application

(Refer to patterned clay fabric, page 34.) Squeeze a layer of the translucent liquid clay over the entire paper transfer image. Apply enough clay to spread it with your fingers into a thin even coat. Extend the clay beyond the image at least ¼" on each side.

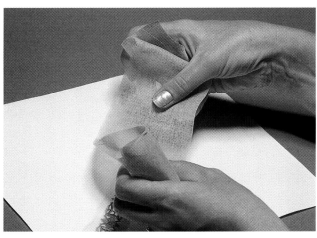

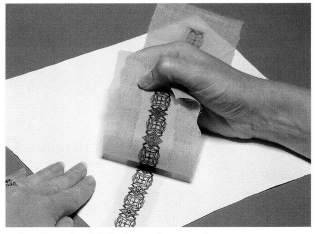

3 • Laying the fabric

Starting from the center of the strip of fabric, carefully lay the well-pressed fabric over the image. The fabric should extend at least ½" over the edges of the image on all sides. Allow the clay to soak through the fabric for a few moments. Starting from the center of the strip and working towards the ends, press the fabric into the liquid clay using even pressure with your fingers. This will remove air pockets. If the fabric is not entirely saturated, squeeze a small amount of liquid clay onto the non-saturated areas and spread it evenly with your fingers. The fabric is saturated when you can see a slight sheen on the side of the fabric that is facing up. Bake the paper and fabric on a flat tray at 265 degrees (F) for 10 minutes. *Tip: A regular toaster oven works best for this, since a convection oven blows air that may disturb the fabric.*

4 • Peeling the fabric from the transfer

Immediately after removing the fabric from the oven (use oven mitts), while the paper and fabric are still hot, peel the fabric away from the transfer image. If it is difficult to peel, try warming the fabric and paper up again, and try a second time. Lay the peeled fabric on a flat surface, and allow it to cool.

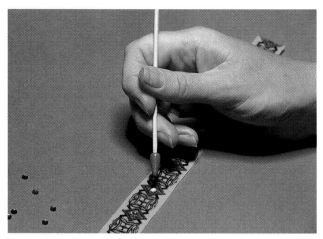

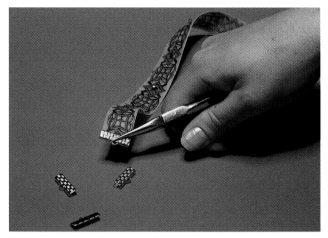

5 • Adding the stones

Once the fabric has been peeled from the paper, turn the fabric face up on a cool baking tray. Place a dot of translucent liquid clay in the center of each design on the transfer image. Pinch a small blob of clay onto the end of a wooden skewer, and shape it into a point. Use the clay tip to pick up one of the glass or crystal flat back rhinestones, and gently place it in the center of the small dot of liquid clay. Repeat for all nine stones. Bake the fabric strip face up at 265 degrees (F) for another 10 minutes. Allow the fabric to cool completely. Bend the fabric strip to check if the stones will stay in place. Any loose stones can be placed back in their liquid clay bezels with a tiny amount of Bond 527 cement. With the ruler, mark the size of the choker (¾" x 12") lightly on the clay fabric with a colored pencil. Cut out the choker.

6 • Adding the choker ends

Place a small dab of E-6000 glue on the very end of the fabric strip (optional). Place the choker clamp over the end, and clamp securely onto the clay fabric with your needle nose pliers, enclosing the end of the strip. Repeat for the other end of the choker.

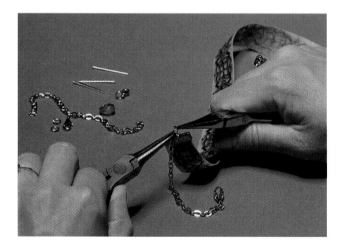

7 • Adding the clasp and extender

On one end of the choker, add the lobster clasp using a jump ring (refer to Adding a clasp, page 42). Attach the extender chain using the same method. Add the beaded drop to the end of the extender (refer to using head pins for drops, page 43). Your choker is complete. The length can be adjusted when worn by hooking the clasp through various loops in the extender chain.

Clay Fabric Purse

MATERIALS&TOOLS

- ⅛ block black Premo
- ⅛ block silver Premo
- 2 pattern pieces, front and back (refer to pattern for clay fabric purse, pages 137 and 138)

- Transfer image for clay fabric purse (page 138)
- 2 pieces of light gold color fabric with a subtle print, light or medium weight, cotton or cotton/polyester blend, well pressed, 9" x 12" each
  - ⅓ yard gold decorative trim, ⅜" wide
  - 1¼ yards gold decorative cording, ⅛" thick
  - Gold and red mix beaded fringe, 6" long piece
  - Dark gray embroidery thread or heavy duty decorative thread
  - 1 set self-adhesive Velcro hook and loop fasteners, ⅝" round
  - 2 gold tone eyelets, ¼"

- 2 red pointed oval glass stones, 6 mm x 10 mm
- 1 red round glass stone, 6 mm
- Liquid polymer clay tool kit (refer to page 18)
- Baking kit (refer to page 17)
- Extra fine point permanent marker
- White oil-based colored pencil
- Scissors
- Craftsman contact cement
- Hole punch, 1mm
- Hole punch, 3mm to 4mm, or leather hole punch with pad and mallet
- Eyelet setting tool, pad, and mallet
- Tapestry needle
- Tissue blade or craft knife

1 • Clay application

Make two copies of the transfer image on a copier that uses toner. (Refer to patterned clay fabric, page 34.) Squeeze a layer of translucent liquid clay over the paper image. Apply enough clay to spread it with your fingers into a thin even coat over the image. Extend the clay beyond the image at least ¼" on each side. Set the first sheet aside, and repeat the clay application for the second transfer sheet.

2 • Laying the fabric

Starting at one edge of the strip of fabric, carefully lay the well-pressed fabric over the image. The fabric should extend at least ½" over the edges of the image on all sides. Allow the clay to soak through the fabric for a few moments. Starting from the center of the strip and working towards the ends, press the fabric into the liquid clay using even pressure with your fingers. This will help remove air pockets. If the fabric is not entirely saturated, squeeze a small amount of liquid clay onto the non-saturated areas and spread it evenly with your fingers. The fabric is saturated when you can see a slight sheen on the side of the fabric that is facing up. Bake the paper and fabric on a flat tray at 265 degrees (F) for 10 minutes, watching closely so the fabric does not burn. Repeat this step for the second image. *Tip: A regular toaster oven works best for this, since a convection oven blows air that may disturb the fabric.*

3 • Peeling the fabric from the transfer

Immediately after removing the fabric from the oven (use oven mitts), while the paper and fabric are still hot, peel the fabric away from the transfer image. If it is difficult to peel, try warming the fabric and paper, and try a second time. Lay the peeled fabric on a flat surface, and allow it to cool. Repeat baking and peeling steps for the second piece of fabric. *Tip: If you are unable to remove all the paper cleanly after several attempts at re-heating, allow the fabric to cool, and then soak it in a basin of water. When the remaining paper is saturated, scrub it off with your fingers and sand lightly with wet sandpaper. If you do soak the fabric, allow it to dry before using it for the project.*

4 • Cut out the purse pattern pieces

Take the larger of the purse pattern pieces, and center it on top of the first clay fabric sheet. Trace the pattern outline using an oil pencil or extra fine point marker. Center the second pattern piece over the second piece of fabric. Outline it carefully. Cut out both purse sections, following just within the traced line of the pattern.

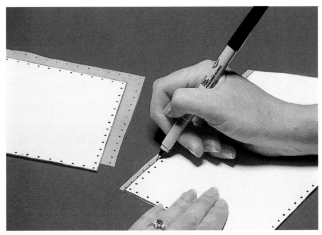

5 • Mark the punch holes

Flip over the larger of the cutout purse pieces, and re-align the pattern piece ⅛" from the edge. Following the markings on the pattern, dot the punch holes on the backside of the fabric with the extra fine point marker. Repeat for the opposite edge and bottom edge of the pouch. Mark the eyelet holes for the purse strap. Repeat marking the punch holes for the second piece of the pouch.

6 • Punch holes

Use a 1mm hole punch to punch out all of the marked holes on both pieces, except for the two purse strap eyelet holes.

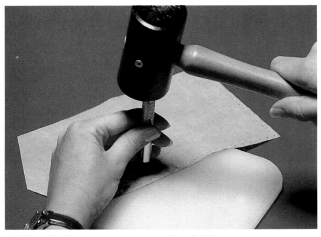

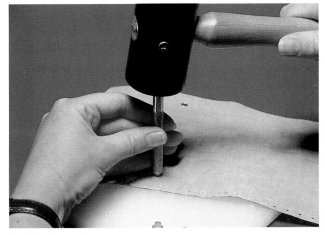

7 • Punch the purse strap eyelet holes

Make sure the protective pad is under the clay fabric and leather punch. Align the 3mm to 4mm leather punch with the eyelet hole markings, and tap firmly with the mallet. These holes can also be made with a 3mm to 4mm hole punch.

8 • Apply eyelets

Make sure the protective pad is under the clay fabric and the leather punch. Turn the clay fabric wrong side up, and insert the eyelet from the bottom (right side) of the clay fabric. Insert the eyelet-setting tool into the center of the eyelet, and strike firmly with the mallet.

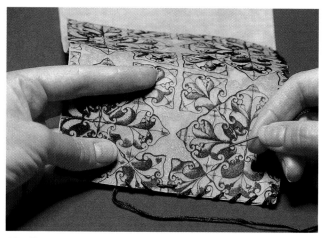

9 · Sew the edges together

Thread the tapestry needle with embroidery or heavy duty thread doubled over, and knot the end. Lay the front and back pieces of the purse together, matching up the punch holes. Starting at the holes at the top of one side of the purse, stitch through the first hole twice to secure the thread. Whip stitch all the way around both pieces to the bottom center of the purse.

10 · Reverse the stitching direction

Take one running stitch to the next hole at the bottom center of the purse, so you can reverse the direction of the whip stitch on the other side of the purse.

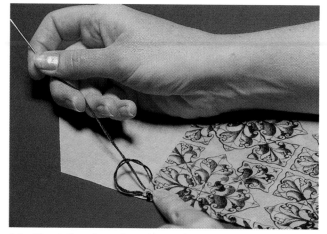

11 · Knot the thread at the end:

When you reach the final hole on the other side, stitch to secure the knot, and clip the thread. You can use a dot of glue on the starting and ending knots to permanently secure the thread.

12 · Attach the beaded fringe

Apply contact cement to the backside of the tape edge on the beaded fringe and the bottom edge of the purse on the flap side. Allow the contact cement to set. Fold under the raw edges of the beaded fringe, trimming off the excess, and press the fringe onto the purse.

13 • Attach the gold trim

Apply contact cement to the bottom edge of the purse, both to the back of the purse and to the front over the tape edge of the fringe. Spread contact cement on the back of the gold decorative trim. Allow the contact cement to set. Press the gold trim all the way around the bottom of the purse, folding the raw edges under and cutting off the excess trim.

14 • Add the strap cording

From the outside of the purse, pull one end of the gold strap cording through each eyelet hole to the inside of the purse, and knot the cord ends. Knot the two sections of the cord together under the purse flap. Center the hook section of the self adhesive Velcro ½" from the tip of the inside of the purse flap, and attach it. Fold over the flap, and mark the center of where the fastener sits on the purse. Attach the loop portion of the Velcro fastener to the purse.

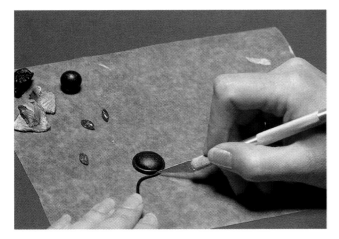

15 • Form the decorative button

Mix the black and silver clays together completely. Form a ½" ball with the clay. Flatten the ball slightly to make a dome. Roll a small piece of clay into a thin snake, and wrap it around the dome to form a decorative edge. Trim the excess clay off where the snake ends meet.

16 • Add the stones

Cover the top of the clay dome with a very thin coat of liquid clay. Press three glass stones into the dome. Bake the clay and stone embellishment for 18 minutes at 275 degrees (F). Allow the button decoration to cool. Place a dot of contact cement in the center of the front of the purse flap, ½" from the tip of the flap, and on the back of the decorative button. Allow the cement to set, and press the clay button onto the flap of the purse. The purse is now complete.

Gallery of Ideas

SECTION 1 • TRANSFERS

Clockwise from top left:

1 "Future Harvest" leaf necklace comprised of liquid clay transfer leaves over solid backings on woven wire.

2 Hand-colored thin sheet liquid clay transfer set in polymer clay frame.

3 Transfer necklace titled "Spring Blossoms." Hand-colored liquid clay transfer applied to a solid clay backing. Transfer has been painted with additional tinted liquid clay and embellished with solid clay and glass cabochons.

4 Dragonfly sculpture titled "Nature's Gem." The wings of the dragonfly are liquid clay transfers adhered to solid polymer clay wings and decorated with glass cabochons.

Clockwise from top left:

1 Lampshades of clay fabric transfers. Most are punched and ribboned onto the lampshades.

2 Clay fabric transfers applied to glass and felt. Clay fabric is adhered to a frame of solid polymer clay for the fan, and the upper edge is gilded with a stripe of gold-tinted liquid clay.

3 Edwardian doll titled "Turn of the Century." The doll's garments have been made entirely from hand-stitched clay fabric embellished with metallic leafed strips of solid polymer clay.

4 "Collar of Faunus." Wired clay fabric transfer leaves that have been woven onto a wire necklace.

5 "Floral Fantasy." Tiny bouquet of clay fabric transfer flowers and leaves in a solid polymer clay vase that has been embellished with a liquid clay fabric transfer.

Chapter 6

Impression Glazing

Motifs

Carved wood and metalwork from Thailand, Indian table. All of the visuals in this chapter introduction demonstrate a richness of texture and design that can be translated into polymer clay.

As our world becomes more technologically advanced, sleek, and computer generated, there is a desire to return to motifs that are earthy, natural, and ancient. Motifs have evolved in a manner similar to imagery in art. Over time repetitive cultural influences solidified into culturally accepted imagery that formed the motifs used for architectural and decorative elements. Most ornament was created by the repetition of a few simple elements; many of these forms were derived from nature. For the Egyptians, the lotus and papyrus symbolized creation and these motifs appeared repeatedly on the decorative objects and architecture of ancient Egypt.[7] A stylized cluster of foliage resembling honeysuckle can often be seen in Greek ornamentation.[8] The Romans showed a prolific use of the acanthus leaf.[9] The Celts added elongated depictions of lizards, birds, and snakes to their designs.[10] In the eighteenth and nineteenth centuries, the science of botany brought the use of less stylized flora to the attention of artists.

As ornamentation evolved, many of these motifs were implemented in a dimensional manner, used in relief, fabric, carving, metalwork, and a multitude of architectural embellishments such as column capitals. Artists of all types can find inspiration in the decorative arts. It is important to pay attention to the feel of a piece and the dimensional aspects of it, be it from depth of color, its hand wrought nature, or organic texture.

Tibetan stamp.

Impression Glazing

Polymer clay artists have been using a wide variety of materials to add texture to solid polymer clay pieces. Liquid polymer clay allows us the added dimension of filling those impressions with clay. For these projects, liquid clay in contrasting colors was used to create the look of an antique piece and to make the textures more visible. Impression glazing can be done with any combination of colors, resulting in a variety of looks.

The first two projects involve stamping the texture onto the clay using leather stamps, rubber stamps, and texturing tools, and then adding color in the texture using liquid clay. On the barrette project, you will be stamping on metallic-leaf-covered clay. This adds richness and depth to the finished piece.

On the second two projects, you will be using natural shells and leaves to make the impressions, giving the projects a more botanical look. It is important to select shells with deep grooves and leaves with raised veins in order to achieve the best result. Translucent clay is used for both projects—for its translucent quality on the leaf votive and its natural appeal on the shell necklace.

Hand wrought silver purse and box from Thailand, Victorian-inspired lamp, Indian sari. Indian ornament, though influenced by the Persians, has its own unique flow. Over the centuries, Indians have specialized in fabric. The term paisley pattern comes from the Scottish imitation of Indian fabrics manufactured in the town of Paisley.[11]

Grape Leaf Textured Barrette

MATERIALS & TOOLS

- ⅓ block Premo: white, purple, cobalt
- Pattern for textured barrette (page 138)
- French barrette, 3¼"
- Basic tool kit (refer to page 17)
- Liquid polymer clay tool kit (refer to page 18)
- Baking kit (refer to page 17)
- Pearl Ex mica pigment powder: duo red-blue, spring green
- Oil paints: ultramarine violet, sap green

- Variegated metallic leaf
- Grape leaf shape leather stamp, ⅝"
- Fimo polymer clay varnish, gloss finish
- Flat brush with a small rounded tip on the handle, ½"
- Brush cleaner
- E-6000 industrial craft adhesive

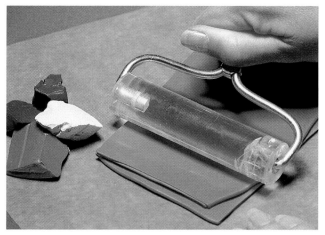

1 • Prepare the clay

Condition all three colors of solid clay. Mix the colors together until thoroughly blended. Roll the clay through the pasta machine into a 5/64" sheet (#3 setting). Cut out two 3½" x 4¾" rectangles. Lay one sheet on top of the other, and use the brayer to roll them together, eliminating air pockets.

2 • Apply gold leaf

Lay the barrette pattern on top of the clay, and trim the rectangle to a diamond shape slightly larger than the pattern. On the work surface covered with wax paper, lay one sheet of variegated gold leaf. Gently place the entire trimmed clay sheet on top of the leaf. Trim off the excess leaf, and save it for another project.

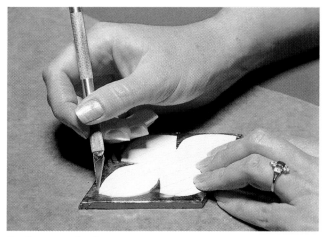

3 • Cut out the barrette

Turn the clay sheet over so the metallic side is up. With a fingertip, gently burnish the leaf onto the surface of the clay. Lay a paper barrette pattern on top of the clay, and cut out the shape.

4 • Stamp texture

Use the leaf leather stamp to make impressions all over the surface of the metallic clay barrette shape. Use the small rounded end of the brush handle to make impressions resembling grape clusters between the leaf impressions.

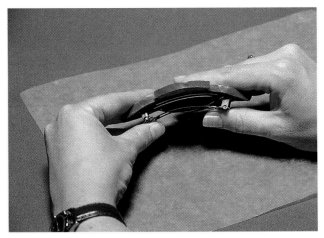

5 • Curve and bake the barrette

Curve the clay to match the curve of the barrette. Place the clay on top of the barrette, and set it gently in the baking pan. Bake the clay on the barrette at 275 degrees (F) for 20 minutes. Allow the clay and barrette to cool completely.

6 • Fill the impressions

In one section of the metal palette, pour ½ teaspoon of translucent liquid Sculpey. With the tip of a skewer, scoop a small dab (the size of a pin head) of sap green oil paint and ¹⁄₁₆ teaspoon of spring green mica pigment powder into the clay. Mix the powder and paint thoroughly. With the tip of your finger or a brush, spread the green liquid clay across the top of the leaf impressions. In a second section of the metal palette, pour ½ teaspoon of translucent liquid clay. Mix a small dab (the size of a pin head) of ultramarine violet paint and ¹⁄₁₆ teaspoon of duo red-blue mica pigment powder into the clay, stirring it in completely with the skewer. With the tip of your finger or a brush, fill the grape impressions with purple liquid clay. Do not rub the liquid clay too vigorously over the surface, or some of the metallic leaf will lift off. Gently wipe the excess clay off the surface of the metallic leaf with your finger. Place the clay barrette shape on top of the barrette in the baking tray. Bake the barrette with clay again at 275 degrees (F) for 10 minutes. Allow the barrette with the clay to cool completely.

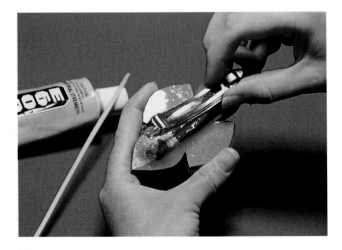

7 • Attach the barrette back

Squeeze a continuous line of glue down the center of the backside of the clay the length of the barrette. Spread glue evenly with the tip of a skewer. Place the barrette into the glue. Allow the glue to dry for 24 hours. Varnish the top surface of the clay to protect the metallic leaf and enhance the colors and shine. Allow the varnish to dry.

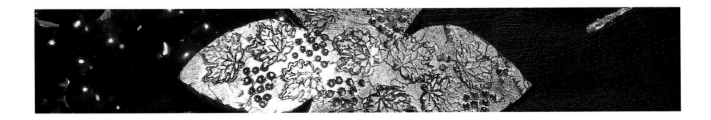

Stamped Magnet Frame

- 1 block leaf green Premo
- ½ block copper Premo
- Basic tool kit (refer to page 17)
- Liquid polymer clay tool kit (refer to page 18)
- Baking kit (refer to page 17)
- 3 oval cutters, 1¼" x 1½", 2" x 2⅜", 2¾" x 3⅜"
- Pearl Ex sparkle gold mica pigment powder
- Rubber stamp
- Magnetic strip or sheet
- E-6000 industrial craft glue
- Fimo polymer clay varnish, gloss finish
- Cornstarch
- Flat brush, ½"
- Soft brush, ½"
- Tape (masking or clear)
- Brush cleaner

1 • Stamp the green clay

Condition the leaf green clay. Roll out a ⅛" thick sheet (#1 setting). Dust the sheet of clay with cornstarch. Using the rubber stamp, stamp randomly over the entire surface of the clay. Press firmly to leave a good impression of the stamp.

3 • Stamp the copper clay

Repeat step 1 using copper clay.

5 • Make the frame

Center the copper oval over the leaf green oval, and press them together. Using the smallest of the oval canapé cutters, cut an oval out of the center to form a frame. Bake the frame for 20 minutes at 275 degrees (F). Cool the frame flat.

2 • Cut the largest oval

Use the largest of the three oval cutters to cut an oval from the stamped sheet of leaf green clay.

4 • Cut the medium oval

Use the medium oval cutter to cut an oval out of the copper clay.

6 • Glaze impressions

In one section of the metal palette, combine ½ teaspoon of liquid clay with ¹⁄₁₆ teaspoon of sparkle gold mica powder. Mix thoroughly with a skewer. Use your finger or a paintbrush to spread a thin coat of liquid clay over the entire surface of the frame. Allow the clay to settle into the impressions made by the stamp. Wipe the excess tinted liquid clay off with a paper towel. Bake the frame for 10 minutes at 275 degrees (F).

7 • Complete the frame

Allow the frame to cool, varnish it with a coat of Fimo varnish, and allow it to dry. Cut four small strips of magnetic strip, and glue them to the back of the frame with E-6000 industrial craft adhesive. Use a skewer to spread the glue. Trim a photo to fit within the magnet edge, and hold it in place with small pieces of tape. Photos can be exchanged and will stay in place once the magnet is on a metal surface or refrigerator.

Shell Necklace

- ¾ block translucent Premo
- ¼ block Premo: tan, white, gold
- ¼" ball leaf green Premo
- Pattern for shell necklace drop (page 138)
- 42 gold 'e' beads
- 16" piece of necklace memory wire
- Basic tool kit (refer to page 17)
- Liquid polymer clay tool kit (refer to page 18)
- Baking kit (refer to page 17)
- Pearl Ex antique bronze mica pigment powder
- Shell for texture
- 12" straight tempered wire
- Heavy wire clippers

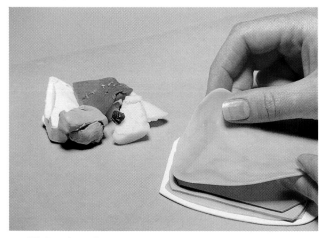

1 • Make clay sheets

Condition all the clay colors. Tint half of the block of translucent clay with the ¼" ball of leaf green clay. Mix the two colors completely until you have a pale green translucent color. Roll out two ¹⁄₁₆" thick sheets (#4 setting) on the pasta machine. Roll out one sheet of tan and one sheet of gold, to ¹⁄₁₆" each (#4 setting). Roll out one ³⁄₆₄" sheet (#5 setting) of white clay. Stack the sheets in the following order starting at the bottom: white, green, tan, gold, green. Roll the sheets together with a brayer.

2 • Make the striped cane

Roll the stacked sheets through the pasta machine to a ⅛" thickness (#1 setting). Roll this sheet so it is ³⁄₃₂" thick (#2 setting) and finally to a thickness of ⁵⁄₆₄" (#3 setting). Cut the sheet into 1" wide strips, and stack them on top of each other to form a striped cane. Brayer the stack to eliminate air pockets.

3 • Make a patterned sheet

Roll the remaining ½ block of translucent clay to a ¹⁄₁₆" thickness (#4 setting). Slice thin strips from the striped cane and lay them onto the translucent sheet, covering the sheet completely. Brayer the slices onto the sheet, and then roll the sheet through the pasta machine first to a ⁵⁄₆₄" thickness (#3 setting) and then to a ¹⁄₁₆" thickness (#4 setting).

4 • Cut out shapes

Using the pattern (placed diagonally across the stripes), cut out five shapes from the prepared striped sheet of clay.

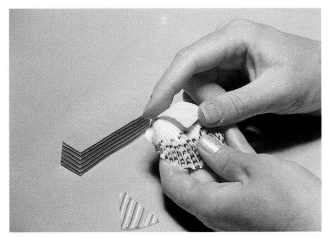

5 • Texture the shapes

Place each shape face down on the shell, and press firmly to give each shape a texture. ***Note:*** *If the clay sticks to the shell, dust a layer of cornstarch onto the shell each time you texture a piece of clay.* Turn over the top ½" of each shape to form a flat loop at the top of each shape, and press the clay together, leaving the loop open enough to string onto a wire. The texture should be on the front, and the loop should fold to the backside of the clay shape. Bake all five shapes for 15 minutes at 275 degrees (F).

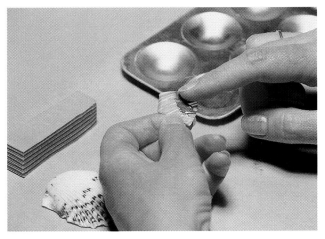

6 • Glaze impressions

In one section of the metal palette, place ½ teaspoon of translucent liquid clay and add ¹⁄₁₆ teaspoon antique bronze mica powder, stirring the powder in completely. Spread the tinted liquid clay over each of the baked clay shapes, allowing the clay to settle into the shell texture. Wipe away the excess liquid clay with a paper towel, leaving some of the tinted clay in the impressions. Bake the clay shapes again for 15 minutes at 275 degrees (F).

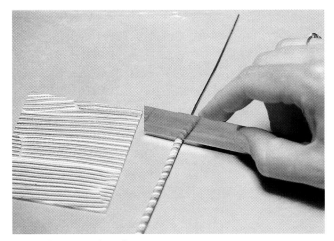

7 • Make extra beads

Roll a ¼" translucent clay snake, and pierce it lengthwise through the center with the 12" piece of straight tempered wire. While still on the wire, roll the snake so that it is ⅛" thick. Roll the striped clay sheet over the snake, and trim it to fit, matching the seams. Carefully roll the clay on the wire to eliminate any air pockets and to blend the seams where the striped sheet meets. Using your tissue blade in a rolling motion, cut ¼" tube beads. You will need about 34 tube beads. Bake the beads on the wire for 15 minutes at 275 degrees (F).

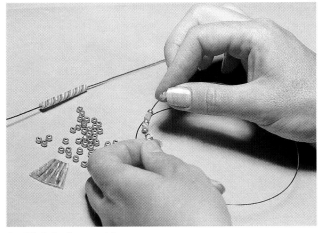

8 • Finish the necklace

Make a loop in one end of a 16" piece of memory wire using your round nose pliers. String the necklace alternating 'e' beads with clay tube beads. Space the five shapes across the front of the necklace with a clay tube bead with an 'e' bead on each end between each shape. Finish the other end of the necklace by making another loop in the memory wire.

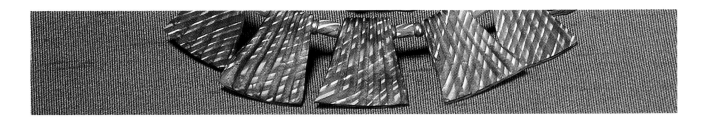

Leaf Votive

MATERIALS&TOOLS

- 1 block translucent Premo
- 2 balls of each color Premo or Sculpey III, ⅛": mint, gold, raw sienna, leaf green
- 2½" glass votive
- 8 or 9 fresh leaves, stiff with good definition on the veins, varied sizes
- Basic tool kit (refer to page 17)
- Liquid polymer clay tool kit (refer to page 18)
- Baking kit (refer to page 17)
- Pearl Ex Aztec gold mica pigment powder

- Oil paint, sap green
- Fimo polymer clay varnish, gloss or matte finish
- Cornstarch
- Flat brush, ½"
- Soft brush, ½"
- Brush cleaner

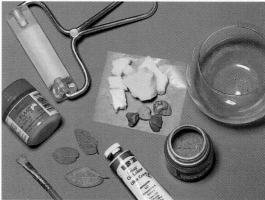

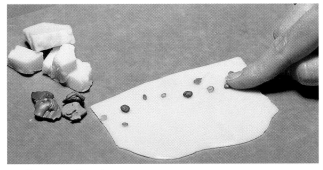

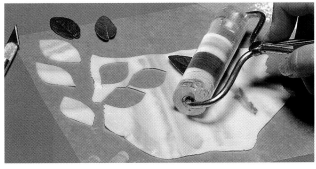

1 • Prepare the clay

Condition the translucent clay. Roll the clay into a ⅛" thick sheet (#1 setting). Place all eight ⅛" balls of conditioned clay on the translucent sheet of clay. Fold the sheet of translucent clay in half. Roll the folded sheet through the pasta machine three or four times at the ⅛" thickness, always folding and rolling the sheet in the same direction. Next roll the sheet through to a 5⁄64" (#3 setting), and then a 3⁄64" thickness (#5 setting). Lay the striped translucent clay sheet on wax paper on your flat work surface.

2 • Cut out the leaves

Trim the stems from the real leaves. Use the ½" soft brush to dust the surface of the clay sheet lightly with cornstarch. Place the leaves all over the sheet of clay, allowing a ¼" between each leaf. Use a brayer to roll the leaves into the clay, making sure not to press too hard and break through the clay sheet. Trim around the leaves, close to the edge. Lift the clay leaves off the wax paper. Remove the real leaves and discard.

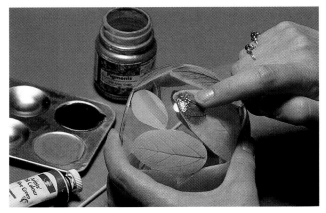

3 • Attach the clay leaves to the votive holder

Turn over one clay leaf, and use your finger to apply a thin layer of translucent liquid polymer clay to the non-textured side. Place the leaf on the side of the votive. Press gently to remove air pockets without disturbing the texture. Repeat this process for adding leaves, allowing some glass to show. When you are pleased with the leaf arrangement, bake the votive holder for 15 minutes at 265 degrees (F). Allow it to cool completely.

4 • Tint the leaves

On the metal palette, squeeze ½ teaspoon of translucent liquid clay. Using a wooden skewer, add a dab (the size of half a pea) of sap green oil paint, and mix it thoroughly into the liquid clay. Use your finger to spread an even coat of green liquid clay over each leaf, but not on the exposed glass. Wipe off the excess with your finger and then a paper towel. Some clay should remain in the leaf impression for contrast.

5 • Glaze the glass

In a second section of the metal palette, squeeze ½ teaspoon of translucent liquid clay. Spoon ⅛ teaspoon of Aztec gold mica powder into the liquid clay and mix thoroughly. With your fingertip, thinly spread a coat of gold liquid clay onto the exposed glass areas and the bottom of the votive holder. A small amount of gold clay can also cover the outer edges of the leaves. Carefully wipe away any drips and excess liquid clay. Bake the votive holder immediately, turning it upside down on the baking sheet lined with wax paper. Bake at 265 degrees (F) for 10 minutes. Cool the votive completely. Trim any extra clay at the upper lip of the votive holder with a craft knife. Be careful not to peel off the thin sheet of clay on the glass. Varnish the entire surface of the votive holder, and allow it to dry. It is now ready for a small candle.

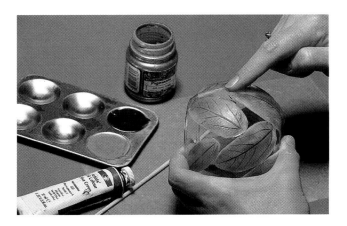

Gallery of Ideas

Clockwise from top left:

1 Three boxes and a journal cover, all textured using rubber stamps and then glazed with tinted liquid clay.

2 Frames, box, and jewelry. Each piece contains elements that have been stamped and glazed. The box is made from a flip, stamp, and fill technique.

3 Variety of refrigerator magnet frames using impression glazing.

4 Detail of flip, stamp, and flip box. Flipped elements have been impressed with leather stamps. This project utilizes metallic leaf for an elegant feel.

5 Flip, stamp, and fill leaf necklace.

Clockwise from top left:

1 Necklace of impression glazed leaf texture on cut out leaf shapes.

2 Liquid clay glazed leaf impressions applied both under and over glass.

3 A picture frame of natural leaf impressions on translucent clay, glazed with liquid clay, and applied over metallic leaf on a liquid clay covered frame.

Chapter 7

Interpretive Imitation

Interpreting the Past

Many types of decorative arts have been passed on through generations, inspiring artists to adapt established techniques to modern materials. The new designs are influenced by the old methods and are given a new spin, still retaining the elements that make the techniques fascinating. The results can echo antiques, yet bring the dying arts into a functional contemporary form. This chapter focuses on two historic decorative arts materials and techniques, mosaics and terra cotta—which are easily reproduced with polymer clay.

Mosaics

The creation of mosaics is the art of arranging colored pieces of marble, glass, stone, tile, wood, or other materials into a fixative to form a surface ornament. Mosaics have been recorded as early as the fourth millennium BC, where cockleshells, onyx, and clay were used to embellish a Sumerian temple.[12] From the fourth century BC, the Greeks completed complex floor mosaics often using natural black and white pebbles as well as glass and stone.[13] Mosaics as we know them today were refined by the Romans, who used small pieces of marble called *tesserae* to reproduce paintings. Some highly detailed examples appear in first century Pompeii.[14] Mosaics developed rapidly in the fourth century AD with the advent of the early Christian wall mosaic. The rapid growth in Christian architecture required a new form of art for the walls. *Tesserae* of colored glass, sometimes with gold backings, were used. This expanded selection of t*esserae* offered a greater range of color and depth than earlier marble work.[15] Mosaics flourished in the Byzantine era, and Christian mosaics continued through the fifteenth century. The Gothic revival of the nineteenth century brought more modern examples like those found in Westminster Abbey.[16]

Italy enjoyed a mosaic revival during the eleventh to thirteenth centuries primarily because of the importation of workers from Greece.[17] Italy is also responsible for another mosaic form, the micromosaic. Micromosaics were developed at the end of the eighteenth century. They were made from tiny *tesserae* called *smalti*. *Smalti* were formed from long filaments of opaque glass that were broken into very short lengths. The *smalti* were set individually into a slow-drying adhesive, the results being a composition as intricate as a painting.[18] These tiny masterpieces were produced primarily for the burgeoning tourist trade of the nineteenth century. Many were purchased as souvenirs while others were exported to other countries to be set in jewelry by local goldsmiths.[19]

From top to bottom:
Modern mosaic tabletop, representing Moroccan style.

Italian micro mosaic of St Mark's Basilica in Venice. The interior is home to many early Italian revival mosaics and St Mark's itself became a site for mosaic workshops.

During the latter half of the nineteenth century, St Peter's Basilica and many of the ancient Roman monuments were the most popular subject matter for micromosaics. Tourists purchased them as souvenirs, much like picture postcards of today.

Terra Cotta

Terra cotta refers to a natural red-brown hard-baked pottery that is used widely for decorative arts and architectural material. Terra cotta was used as an art material for vases and statuettes in Egypt, Persia, Pre-Columbian Central America, and China as early as 3000 BC.[20] The process of making pottery was refined in Mesopotamia. Ceramic objects have been created in almost every ancient society. Terra cotta as a building material was used extensively during the Renaissance. In the fifteenth century, the Italians enameled terra cotta sculptures and relief. Ceramic tile was established in Spain for architectural embellishment in the eleventh century. Spanish methods were transmitted to Mexico by the conquistadors. A distinctive Mexican style was established in the sixteenth to eighteenth centuries.[21]

Interpretive Imitation

Because of its versatility, polymer clay has been used for many types of imitative techniques. Over the centuries, many different styles of mosaics and terra cotta pieces have emerged. Decorative items in these techniques and materials can be found anywhere from bathrooms to gardens. This chapter explores the adaptation of solid and liquid polymer clay to the art of mosaics and terra cotta tiles.

The first two projects in this chapter cover mosaics. Liquid polymer clay can be used as a tile fixative on both solid polymer clay and other materials. Tinted liquid clay is an effective and easily applied grout for mosaics. The first project, the star pin, uses pre-baked solid polymer clay tiles on a polymer clay base. The second project uses raw solid polymer clay tiles adhered to a wooden candlestick. Polymer clay tiles can be made using veneers of enormous diversity, allowing the artist an infinite number of possibilities of finished effects. Both of these projects use double sided veneers that make the mosaic process quicker and easier. The grout on the second project also acts as a patina for the candlestick.

Above: A vase and three small terra cotta pots from Thailand and a terra cotta vase from Germany. Modern day terra cotta pieces can be found all over the world.

The second two projects in this chapter focus on creating realistic-looking terra cotta. The terra cotta Sculpey, manufactured by Polyform, is used to give a real terra cotta feel. Originally inspired by handmade Mexican tiles, each project teaches a different molding technique. The first project, the bracelet, involves making two molds from a leather stamp in order to produce double-sided beads. The picture frame project shows how to carve your own mold. In both projects, the terra cotta elements are glazed with liquid polymer clay to complete the ceramic look.

Left: Today one can find a wide variety of engraved, molded, and painted terra cotta tile from Mexico. All of these styles can serve as excellent inspirations for polymer clay work.

Mosaic Star Pin

MATERIALS & TOOLS

- ½ block Premo: medium red brilliant, white
- 1 block ultramarine Premo
- Pin back, ¾"
- Basic tool kit (refer to page 17)
- Liquid polymer clay tool kit (refer to page 18)
- Baking kit (refer to page 17)
- Pearl Ex silver mica pigment powder
- Star shaped cutter, 2¼"
- Fimo polymer clay varnish, gloss finish
- Flat brush, ½"

- Brush cleaner
- Optional: Fine grade wet/dry sandpaper, 600 and 800 grit

1 • Cut out the star base

Condition the block of ultramarine clay. Roll out a 5/64" thick sheet (#3 setting). Cut the sheet in half; place one sheet on top of the other. Use a brayer to roll the two sheets together, removing air pockets. Cut out a star shape for the pin base. Set aside the star pin base, and save the ultramarine scrap clay.

2 • Layer red and white sheets

Condition the red and white clays. Roll each color into a 1/8" thick sheet (#1 setting). Cut a 2" x 4" rectangle out of the white sheet. Place the white rectangle on top of the red sheet and trim the red clay sheet to the same size. Gently use the brayer to stick the two sheets together.

3 • Create a striped stack

Take the stacked rectangle of red and white, and roll it into a 1/8" thick sheet (#1 setting). Roll the two-colored sheet through a second time to make the sheet 3/32" thick (#2 setting). Cut the rectangle into four equal pieces, 2" wide, and stack the pieces so that the colors alternate. This will create a striped stack. Trim the edges of the stack on all four sides with a tissue blade.

4 • Make the striped sheet

Roll out the remaining scraps of ultramarine clay to a 1/8" thick sheet (#1 setting). Cut off a 1" strip from the sheet and set it aside (this will be used to attach the pin back later). Next roll the remaining ultramarine sheet to a thickness of 5/64" (#3 setting), and finally roll it into a 3/64" thick sheet (#5 setting). Lay the ultramarine sheet of clay in front of you on a piece of wax paper. Cut 1/16" slices off of the red-and-white-striped stack, and place them on the ultramarine sheet, leaving no space between the slices. The stripes should blend together, with none of the ultramarine base sheet showing. Use the brayer to integrate the thin slices into the sheet. With the stripes perpendicular to the roller, roll the sheet of stripes through the pasta machine on a #3 setting and then on a #5 setting. Lay the thin sheet of clay (ultramarine on one side and red and white stripes on the other) into a flat baking pan. Bake the sheet at 275 degrees (F) for 15 minutes, and cool it between two sheets of wax paper under a book or heavy object so the sheet is completely flat. You now have a two-sided sheet that can be used for both the solid ultramarine and the red-and-white-striped tiles.

Interpretive Imitation • 81

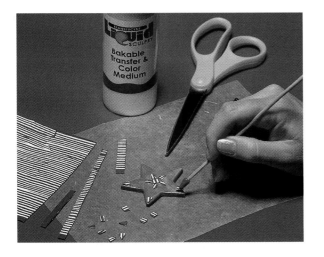

5 • Cut and place the tiles

When the sheet is cool, cut six strips ¼" wide, perpendicular to the stripes. Angling the scissors, cut triangular tiles from the strips. Also cut one square tile for the center of the star and twenty narrow (³⁄₁₆" x ¼") strips for the star outline. Cut enough triangles to cover the entire star (about 35), plus five or six extras. Coat the surface of the star with a thin layer of translucent liquid polymer clay. Place the square tile in the very center of the star, striped side facing up. Outline the center tile with five triangular striped tiles, to form a star in the center of the pin. Align the center star points with the points of the larger star base. Place a triangular striped tile at each outer tip of the star. Use the twenty narrow striped rectangular tiles to outline the edge of the star base. Fill in the remaining space on the star with ultramarine triangles, leaving very little space between tiles. Tiles can be trimmed with scissors to fill in the smaller spaces. When the surface is completely covered, bake the pin for 20 minutes at 275 degrees (F). Cool the star completely.

6 • Grout the pin

Squeeze ½ teaspoon of translucent liquid clay onto a metal palette. Using the end of a skewer, place ⅛ teaspoon of silver mica pigment powder into the clay, and mix it in thoroughly. Using a finger or a brush, fill the gaps between tiles with silver liquid clay. Wipe the excess liquid clay from the surface of the pin with a paper towel and then your finger, exposing the tile surfaces clearly. Bake the pin at 275 degrees (F) for 10 minutes, and allow the pin to cool.

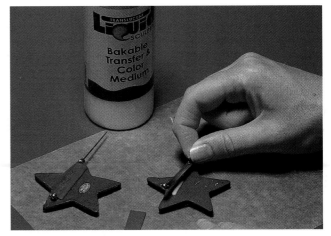

7 • Add the pin back

Using your craft knife, carefully trim the tiles that extend beyond the edge of the clay base. It is optional to wet sand the surface of the mosaic with very fine sandpaper of several grades, ending with 800 grit or higher. Attach pin back. (Refer to the tips section, Attaching pin backs, page 22.) When the pin has been baked and cooled, brush the surface of the mosaic pin with a coat of gloss or matte polymer clay varnish. Allow the pin to dry.

Mosaic Candlestick

MATERIALS & TOOLS

- 1 block turquoise Premo
- Wooden candlestick
- Copper metallic leaf
- Basic tool kit (refer to page 17)
- Liquid polymer clay tool kit (refer to page 18)
- Baking kit (refer to page 17)
- Pearl Ex mica pigment powder: red russet, duo blue-green, duo green-yellow
- Wire mesh or other texture sheet, 4" x 6"
- Stiff brush, ¾"
- Soft flat brush, ½"

- Heat gun (not shown with materials)

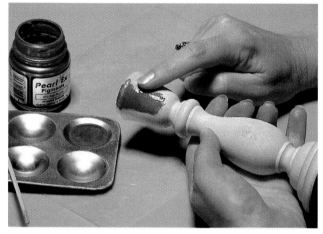

1 • Paint the first coat

In a small glass dish, mix 2 teaspoons of translucent liquid clay with ⅛ teaspoon red russet mica powder. Using a flat brush or your fingertip, cover the wood candlestick completely with a layer of tinted liquid clay (the candlestick can be pre-baked to remove moisture; refer to Materials preparation, page 44). Bake the coated candlestick for 10 minutes at 275 degrees (F).

2 • Add patina

In one section of the metal palette, mix ½ teaspoon translucent liquid clay with ¹⁄₁₆ teaspoon duo blue-green mica powder. Using a stiff brush, stipple the blue-green clay over the red russet clay in a random manner, creating a textural patina look. Bake the candlestick again for 10 minutes at 275 degrees (F).

3 • Prepare the tile sheet

Condition the block of turquoise Premo. Roll out a ⁵⁄₆₄" thick sheet (#3 setting). On one side of the sheet, cover the clay with copper leaf, burnishing it onto the clay with your finger. Roll the sheet through the pasta machine to a ¹⁄₁₆" thickness (#4 setting), and then a ³⁄₆₄" thickness (#5 setting) to crackle the leaf.

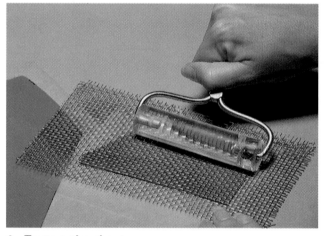

4 • Texture the sheet

Turn the clay sheet so that the turquoise side is facing up. Lay the wire mesh or other texture sheet over the clay and brayer over it. Use a fairly fine texture so that it will be visible when the clay is cut into small tiles.

5 • Cut the tiles

Cut the clay sheet into ¼" strips (the width of the strips can vary depending on the size of the candlestick and the type of mosaic pattern you wish to make). Cut the strips into squares and isosceles triangles (two equal sides). Flip over half of the tiles so that you now have two colors of tiles.

6 • Place the tiles

Select the areas on the candlestick to be covered with tiles. Cover the first area with a thin layer of translucent liquid clay. Place the tiles over the area in a pattern. The unbaked tiles are easier to use on the curved surfaces. Once an area is covered, bake the candlestick for 15 minutes at 275 degrees (F). Repeat this step until all areas are covered. Mosaic tiles can be quickly set in place using a heat gun. Aim the heat at the tiles to set the liquid clay underneath. Keep the heat moving and do not get the gun too close to the tiles or they can be scorched. Clay must still be baked after setting with the heat gun.

7 • Grout the tiles

In another section of the metal palette, mix ½ teaspoon of translucent liquid polymer clay with ¹⁄₁₆ teaspoon of duo green-yellow mica powder for the grout. With your finger, spread the liquid clay over the tiles in each mosaic section on the candlestick. Allow the clay to settle between the tiles. Wipe off the excess with a paper towel. Bake for 15 minutes at 275 degrees (F).

Terra Cotta Bracelet

M
A
T
E
R
I
A
L
S
&
T
O
O
L
S

- ½ block medium red brilliant Premo
- 1 block terra cotta Sculpey
- 9 silver colored 2" eye pins
- 1 silver-colored clasp
- 1 silver-colored ³⁄₁₆" jump ring
- 1 silver-colored ¼" jump ring
- Basic tool kit (refer to page 17)
- Liquid clay tool kit (refer to page 18)
- Baking kit (refer to page 17)
- Oil paint: white, blue, yellow
- Flower shape leather impression tool, ½"

- Cornstarch
- Soft brush, ½"

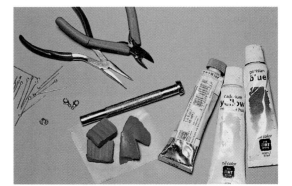

1 • Make the bead molds

Condition the red clay (not terra cotta). Roll it into a ⅝" diameter snake. Cut off two ⅝" slices, and roll them to form ⅝" balls. Flatten the balls to a ¼" thickness. Use the ½" soft brush to dust the flattened surfaces of the balls with cornstarch. Use the leather stamp to make a fairly deep impression on one of the flattened balls. Make the same impression on the second flattened ball. Bake the stamped clay impressions for 20 minutes at 275 degrees (F). Allow the molds to cool.

2 • Mold the beads

Roll the conditioned terra cotta clay into a ½" diameter snake. *Note: The terra cotta Sculpey is very soft, and it will require very little conditioning.* Cut off nine ½" thick slices from the snake. Roll each slice into a ½" ball. Lightly dust each side of the impression molds with cornstarch each time you make a bead. Hold one mold with the impression facing up. Center one ball of clay over the mold. Place the second mold face down over the ball of clay, aligning the impression with that of the bottom mold. Gently press the molds together, sandwiching the terra cotta clay between the molds. Do not squeeze the clay out beyond the edges of the impressions. The two molds with terra cotta clay in between should have the look of a sandwich cookie.

3 • Insert the eye pins

Before removing the clay from the molds, pierce the bead through the center with an eye pin to form the bead hole. Remove the bead from the molds, and repeat for the next eight balls of terra cotta clay. Leave the eye pin in the beads during baking. Bake the beads for 18 minutes at 275 degrees (F), and allow them to cool.

4 • Glaze the beads

In one section of the metal palette, squeeze ½ teaspoon of translucent liquid clay. With the tip of a skewer, place a small dab (the size of a pin head) of white paint and a tiny dot (just what covers the flat tip of the skewer) of yellow paint into the liquid clay and mix it in thoroughly. In the second section of the palette, squeeze ½ teaspoon of translucent liquid clay, and mix in a small dab (the size of a pin head) of white and a tiny dot of blue oil paint. Use a finger to wipe a coat of pale yellow liquid clay over the front of five beads. With your finger or a paper towel, remove the excess liquid clay, allowing the color to remain in the impressions. For the other four beads, apply the blue liquid clay in the same way, to accent the impressions on one side of the beads. Bake the beads at 275 degrees (F) for 10 minutes. Once the beads have cooled, repeat the coloring process, using the same color on the back as you did on the front of each bead. Bake for another 10 minutes and cool the beads again.

5 • Assemble and finish the bracelet

Pick up one yellow bead, and slide the eye pin so the loop is flush with the side of the bead. With pliers, form a loop on the other side of the bead. Trim the excess of the eye pin with the wire clippers. Before closing the loop with the pliers, hook on the loop of the next eye pin with a blue bead on it. Close the first loop, and repeat the loop process for the second bead. Alternate bead colors. When the bracelet is just slightly longer than a snug fit on the wrist, close the last eye pin loop. Attach the clasp (refer to Adding a clasp, page 42).

Terra Cotta Picture Frame

MATERIALS&TOOLS

- 1 block ecru Premo
- 1½ blocks terra cotta Sculpey
- 1" wide, flat, unfinished wooden picture frame for a 4" x 6" photo
- Transfer for carved tile on frame (page 138)
- Pearl Ex red russet mica pigment powder
- Basic tool kit (refer to page 17)
- Liquid polymer clay tool kit (refer to page 18)
- Baking kit (refer to page 17)
- Oil paints: white, yellow, blue
- Beveled edge metal carving tool or

- craft knife
- Pointed wooden stick
- 1 flat-edged wooden tool or bone folder
- Flower shaped leather stamp, ⅝"
- Leaf shaped leather stamp, ½"
- Cornstarch
- Soft brush, ½"
- Flat brush, ½"
- E-6000 industrial craft glue

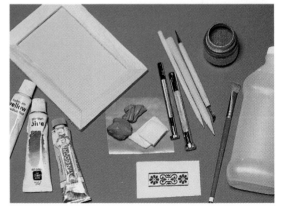

1 • Burnish the transfer image

Condition the entire block of ecru clay. Roll it into a ⅛" thick sheet (#1 setting). Cut the rectangle in half and stack the two halves. Use the brayer to attach the two layers and remove air pockets. Trim to a 2" x 3" rectangle. Make a copy of the transfer image on a copier that uses toner (include a ½" edge). Lay the image ink side down centered on the clay rectangle. Gently burnish the paper onto the clay using the flat-edged wooden tool or bone folder.

2 • Transfer the image onto the clay

Using the brush, saturate the backside of the transfer image with rubbing alcohol. Allow the paper to dry. Burnish the paper once again. Brush on a second coat of alcohol, saturating the paper a second time.

3 • Remove the paper

While still saturated, gently peel back a corner of the paper to check that the image has transferred. If not, allow the paper to dry, burnish again, and saturate a third time. When the image has clearly transferred to the clay, peel away the paper. If the toner is slightly sticky, use the soft brush to dust the image with a light coating of cornstarch.

4 • Carve the transfer image

With the beveled edge metal tool or a craft knife, carve away the parts of the image that do not have ink. Remove the excess clay, and pat down the carved area with the pointed wooden tool. After the tile has been carved, trim the edges of the tile with a tissue blade. Bake the carved tile at 275 degrees (F) for 20 minutes. Allow the tile mold to cool completely. *Note: Real terra cotta tiles are seldom perfect. Do not be concerned that the carved areas be perfectly smooth and even.*

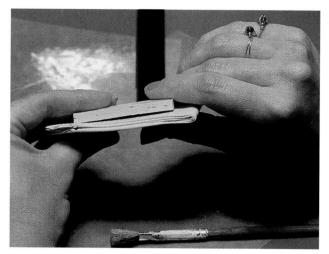

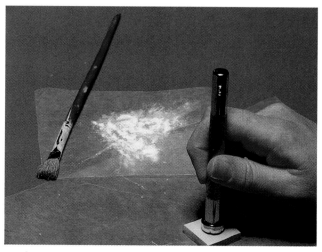

5 • Create the reverse mold

Roll the remaining ecru clay into a ⅛" thick sheet (#1 setting). Cut the rectangle in half and stack the two halves. Roll them together with the brayer. Make sure the ¼" thick rectangle is slightly larger than your mold. Brush your carved mold lightly with cornstarch. Press the rectangle of clay into the mold and over the edges of the mold using your thumbs. This will form the reverse mold. Remove the clay, set it on a flat baking sheet, and bake it for 20 minutes at 275 degrees (F). Allow the clay to cool. You will use this reverse mold to make your larger frame tiles.

6 • Stamp shapes for the smaller molds

Make two smaller 1" squares of ecru clay ¼" thick (double layer of #1 setting). Use the soft brush to dust each square with a light layer of cornstarch. Make a good impression of the flower leather stamp on the first square. Make a leaf impression with the leather stamp on the second square.

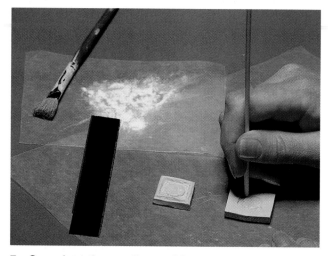

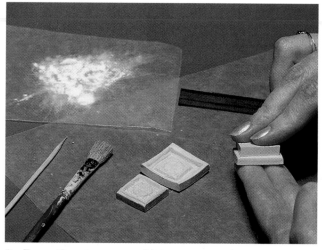

7 • Complete the smaller molds

Use the flat end of a wooden skewer to flatten the clay around the flower impression. Form a square shape around the flower, and then trim the edge of the tile ⅛" from the outside of the square indentation. This will form the edge of the tile. Repeat this step for the leaf stamp. Bake both molds at 275 degrees (F) for 20 minutes. Allow the molds to cool.

8 • Form the reverse molds

Make two 1¼" squares of ecru clay ¼" thick (double layer of #1 setting) to use for your reverse molds. Dust each square lightly with cornstarch. Press the flower mold into the first square to form the reverse mold. Repeat this step with the leaf mold. Bake both reverse molds at 275 degrees (F) for 20 minutes. Allow the reverse molds to cool.

9 • Mold all the frame tiles

Condition the terra cotta clay (it will take very little conditioning), and roll it into a ⁵⁄₆₄" thick sheet (#3 setting). Cut the sheet in half, layer it, and use the brayer to roll the sheets together. Cut the sheet into four rectangles 1" x 2¼", eight 1" squares, and four ¾" squares. Make sure to dust the mold lightly with cornstarch when molding each tile. Using your thumbs, press one of the 1" x 2¼" terra cotta clay rectangles into the reverse mold of the carved transfer mold. Remove the terra cotta clay from the mold and trim the edges of the tile. Repeat for the other three rectangles of the same size. Repeat the same process using the reverse mold of the flower on the eight 1" squares and with the leaf reverse mold on the four ¾" squares. When all 16 tiles have been molded, bake the tiles at 275 degrees (F) for 18 minutes. Allow all tiles to cool.

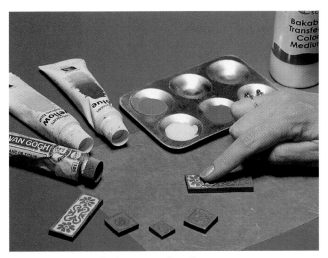

10 • Apply tinted glazes to the tiles

Pour ½ teaspoon of translucent liquid Sculpey into each of three sections on a metal palette. Take a small dab (the size of a pin head) of white oil paint, and mix this into the first section. Repeat for the other two sections. In the first section, add a small dot (just what covers the flat tip of a skewer) of blue oil paint and mix it into the tinted white liquid clay. To the second section, add a slightly smaller dot of blue clay and a small dot of yellow oil paint. Mix the colors thoroughly to make a medium green. In the third section of tinted white clay, add a small dot of yellow oil paint to slightly tint the white to a soft yellow. With the tip of your finger, spread a coat of pale yellow clay over one of the larger rectangular tiles. Remove the excess clay with a fingertip and then with a paper towel, leaving tinted clay in the impressions for contrast. Repeat for the other three rectangular tiles. Use the same glazing method for the flower and leaf tiles, applying the blue glaze to the flower tiles and the green glaze to the leaf tiles. Once all the tiles are glazed, bake them for 10 minutes at 275 degrees (F). Allow the tiles to cool.

11 • Color the frame

In a small glass dish, pour 2 teaspoons of translucent liquid clay. Add ⅛ teaspoon of red-russet mica powder, and stir it in completely with a skewer. Use your finger to spread a thin coat of tinted red-russet liquid clay over the entire frame surface, including the inside and outside edges (the frame can be pre-baked to remove moisture; refer to Materials preparation, page 44). Bake the frame at 265 degrees (F) for 10 minutes, and allow it to cool. Remove the glass and the backing from the frame before baking. Supervise the baking of the frame to keep the wood from burning.

12 • Apply the tiles

Lay the frame flat on your work surface. Apply an even coat of E-6000 industrial craft glue to the back of the first tile. Place the tile carefully on the frame. Starting at the center and working outwards on the frame edge can help center the larger rectangular tiles. Apply the remaining tiles with the craft adhesive. Allow the tiles on the frame to dry on a flat surface for 24 hours, and then add your favorite picture.

Gallery of Ideas

SECTION 1 • MOSAICS

Clockwise from top left:

1 "Roman Revival." This interesting necklace is comprised of small square tiles on a solid polymer clay base.

2 A variation on mosaics, all of these pieces include image transfer solid polymer clay tiles. Some of the mosaics are tiled in such a way that the image remains intact.

3 Home décor and jewelry mosaics constructed of solid polymer clay tiles over papier-mâché, metal, wood, and polymer clay have been adhered, patinated, and grouted with liquid clay.

4 Various colorful mosaics utilizing some metallic leafed and marbled solid clay tiles.

5 Mica mosaic tiles. The tiles on these mosaics are made from thin sheets of liquid polymer clay mixed with mica flakes. The sheets are cut into tiles and then, in the case of these pieces, adhered to glass.

Clockwise from above:

1 Detail of terra cotta tiles. One has been made into a brooch or pendant with terra cotta bead drops.

2 Terra cotta jewelry. Jewelry constructed from terra cotta tiles or elements made from carved or stamped molds. All pieces are glazed with liquid polymer clay.

3 Carved and molded terra cotta tiles on a picture frame, box, and terra cotta flower pots.

Chapter 8

Surface Decoration

Marbled endpapers from three books from the late 1800s. The top book shows combing. The others show a stone veined technique.

Dimensional Details

Whether it is from glasswork or painting, ornate surface decoration adds a spectacular finishing touch to any art project. Surface decoration can be imitative, or it can find its own artistic form.

Marbling

Marbling is the art of floating ink or paint on water, creating a design with it, and then "lifting" the design onto paper, fabric, or another workable material. Examples of Japanese paper marbling, called *Suminagashi*, appear as early as 800 AD.[22] In this technique, ink or ground pigment was floated on water and then blown to form smoke-like patterns.[23] In the fifteenth century, marbling appeared in Turkey and Persia where they used oil paints floated on water thickened with size. The Turks developed the use of combs to pull through the paint to make patterns.[24] Marbling spread to the west in the seventeenth century. The marbled paper was predominantly used as endpapers for bookbinding and occasionally as a backdrop for a coat of arms. Book edges were sometimes marbled so that if any pages were removed from a book it would be immediately evident by the break in the marbled pattern.[25] Over the centuries, more vibrant colors and better sizing materials have been developed, and marbling has been used as a technique for fabric as well. Distinctive patterns have been developed that can be attributed to the styles of different countries.

Fiorato

"Fiorato" or flowered beads are one of the most popular types of Venetian glass beads. These beads are distinguished by a three-dimensional pattern of decorative scrolls and roses, often accentuated by the sparkle of aventurine glass. The elegant and refined look of this type of bead is the result of a substantial history of glass bead making. A forerunner to glass beads, made from a material called faience, appeared in Mesopotamia and Egypt around 4000 BC. Glass beads were being made by 2181 BC. Around 1350 BC, glass bead making in Egypt increased dramatically. Many of the beads were made using complex techniques including layering glass over a sand core.[26] From 800 BC to 200 BC, the Phoenicians (now Lebanon) manufactured and traded wound glass beads that included a considerable amount of surface detail made from successive layers of colored glass.[27] The Chinese also layered glass as a surface decoration on beads to produce the complex geometric patterns of the eye beads from the Warring States period, 481 BC to 221 BC.[28] Glass beads with surface decoration were also prevalent in the Islamic world from 700–1400 AD.[29]

The glass bead industry grew from the Renaissance to the twentieth century primarily for the purpose of trade. Bead makers benefited from the very high profit margins, sometimes as high as 1,000%. After the decline of the western Asian bead strongholds, the Venetian manufacturers became the premier glass bead makers of the Western world.[30] The factories in Murano (which were moved to the island in 1292 due to the risk of fire from the furnaces) produced mostly millefiori and drawn beads. Lampworking, because it required only small oil lamps or torches, was concentrated more in Venice starting in the late 1500s. By 1764 there were 22 Venetian manufacturers producing 44,000 pounds of beads a week.[31]

Venetian fiorato beads get their elegant floral patterns from small molten canes of colored and transparent glass trailed and scrolled in a controlled fashion on the surface of the bead. Another key element on many fiorato beads is the use of aventurine. Also called "stellaria" or star-covered, aventurine is the name given to the copper-gold glass used. A complicated and unpredictable process involving the formation and fusion of copper crystals is used to make aventurine. Its use dates back to the seventeenth century.[32]

Surface Decoration

Because of its viscous and slightly sticky nature, liquid polymer clay lends itself well to both marbling and fiorato techniques. It offers the artist a broader range of options for detailing the surface of both polymer and mixed media projects. The first two projects in this chapter are marbling techniques. Nan Roche has explored traditional marbling techniques with liquid polymer clay. She floats liquid polymer clay tinted with pigments of various types on water, combs or swirls a pattern into the clay, and lifts the marbled pattern from the surface of the water with a sheet of solid polymer clay. The results vary, depending on the types of pigments used to tint the liquid clay.

In this chapter, you will be marbling by laying down stripes and dots of tinted liquid clay on a solid clay base and then combing through them using a skewer or pin tool. On the earring project, most of the surface area is marbled. On the clock, only the leaf elements are marbled. Marbling offers a colorful and captivating finish and an interesting option for your polymer clay work.

The unique properties of liquid polymer clay allow the polymer clay artist to imitate fiorato and lampwork beads with surprising accuracy. Liquid clay can be used to mimic the suspended copper sparkle of aventurine, and the clay scrolls well, with soft edges, much like the look of molten glass. Polymer cannot duplicate the look of transparent glass, but a tinted translucent base, decorated with liquid clay trailings and sealed with a gloss varnish, gives the depth and feel of opaque glass. This process also has the advantage of not requiring torches or dangerous equipment, and the resulting beads are much lighter in weight. The first of the two fiorato projects in this chapter is for fiorato beads; the second is for a fiorato-glass-inspired vase. The method of scrolling liquid clay used for fiorato can be used on other types of projects as well, so let your imagination take flight.

Above and Opposite Bottom: Examples of Venetian fiorato bead necklaces and a bracelet.

Marbled Earrings

MATERIALS&TOOLS

- ½ block gold Premo
- 2 earring posts
- 2 earring nuts
- Basic tool kit (refer to page 17)
- Liquid polymer clay tool kit (refer to page 18)
- Baking kit (refer to page 17)
- Pearl Ex mica pigment powders: duo red-blue, sparkle gold, brilliant yellow
- Oil paints: sap green, ultramarine violet
- Fine heat-resistant copper glitter

- Gildenglitz variegated metallic leaf flakes
- Oval cutter, ¾" x 1"
- Small square cutter, ½"
- Pin tool
- Fimo polymer clay varnish, gloss finish
- Flat brush, ½"
- Brush cleaner

1 • Roll the clay and add the leaf

Condition the gold clay and roll it into a ⅛" thick sheet (#1 setting). Cut the rectangle in half. Set one half of the clay sheet aside. Apply a coating of variegated leaf flakes to the second half, covering the clay completely. Burnish the leaf onto the clay with your finger.

2 • Cut the earring shapes

Cut two ovals from the plain gold clay rectangle. Cut two small squares from the piece of clay covered in leaf.

3 • Attach the shapes

With a fingertip, spread a very thin layer of translucent liquid clay over the surface of each oval. On top of one oval, place one of the small squares oriented with the corners aligned with the length of the oval. With the metallic leaf side facing up, press the square gently onto the oval to adhere. Repeat for the second oval. Bake the earring bases at 275 degrees (F) for 18 minutes. Allow the earrings to cool.

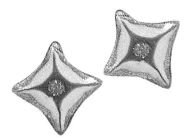

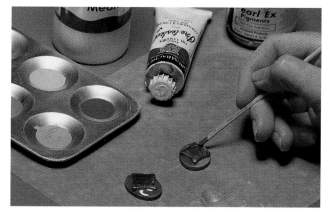

4 • Mix the liquid clay colors

In the metal palette, squeeze ½ teaspoon of liquid clay into each of four sections. In the first section, use the tip of the skewer to mix a small dab (the size of a pin head) of ultramarine violet oil paint into the liquid clay. Use the paper towel to wipe the skewer each time you add a new color. Add ⅛ teaspoon of duo red-blue mica powder to the ultramarine violet tinted liquid clay. In the second section on the palette, add a small dab of sap green oil paint into the translucent liquid clay. Next add ¹⁄₁₆ teaspoon of sparkle gold mica powder to the tinted sap green clay. In the third section, add ⅛ teaspoon of brilliant yellow mica powder to the translucent clay. To the fourth section, add ⅛ teaspoon of copper glitter to the translucent liquid clay. Make sure all colors are mixed completely. On one earring base, at each of the four edges of the oval outside the square center, put a drop of translucent liquid clay, and spread it into a thin layer over the earring base. Use the skewer to place a drop of purple clay on each of these four sections. With the pointed tip of the skewer, spread the purple clay over the entire surface of each section. Repeat on the second earring base.

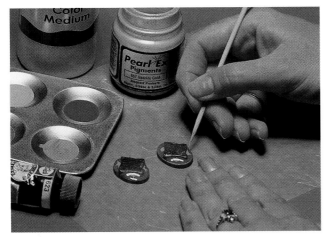

5 • Add the green-gold clay details

With the pointed tip of the skewer, place a small drop of green-gold tinted liquid clay in the center of one purple section. Use the skewer point to drag the green-gold color through the purple in three places. Repeat for the other three sections. Make sure to wipe the pin tool with the paper towel each time you drag the color. Repeat the green dots and dragging on the second earring. Bake the earring bases for 10 minutes at 275 degrees (F), and allow the earrings to cool.

6 • Add the yellow clay

For the center of the earring, start by wiping a very thin layer of untinted translucent clay over the variegated leafed square with your fingertip. Using the flat end of the wooden skewer, place a drop of yellow tinted clay onto the square. Repeat for the second earring.

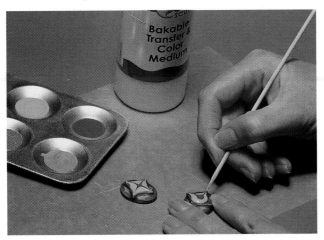

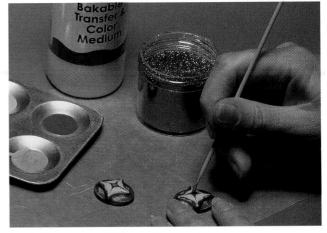

7 • Add the purple clay details to the center

Place a slightly smaller drop of purple clay in the center of the square on top of the yellow clay. Use the skewer point to drag the purple clay to each of the corners of the square through the yellow clay.

8 • Add copper glitter to the center

Use the skewer to drop a small dot of copper glitter clay in the center of the purple and yellow clay. Repeat steps 7 and 8 for the second earring center. Bake the earrings at 275 degrees (F) for 10 minutes, and allow them to cool.

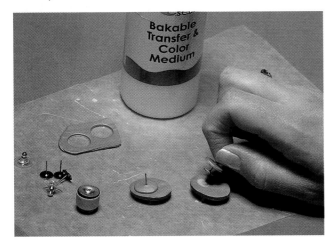

9 • Finish and varnish

Attach earring posts to the backs of the earrings. (Refer to Attaching earring posts, page 23.) When the earrings have cooled, use the flat brush to apply a coat of polymer clay gloss varnish to the surface of the earrings. Allow them to dry. The earrings are now ready to wear.

Marbled Clock

MATERIALS & TOOLS

- 3 blocks gold Premo
- ½ block green Premo
- Clock movement and hands kit
- 1 AA battery
- 4 dark red faceted glass cabochons, 10mm x 13 mm
- Basic tool kit (refer to page 17)
- Liquid polymer clay tool kit (refer to page 18)
- Baking kit (refer to page 17)
- Oil paints: red, black

- Pearl Ex mica pigment powders: red russet, spring green, pearl white
- Glitter, gold iridescent (heat resistant)
- Round cutter, ⅜"
- Three-pointed leaf cutter, 1" x 1¼"
- Metal ruler
- Polymer clay varnish, gloss finish
- Flat brush, ¼"
- Brush cleaner

1 • Prepare the base of the clock

Condition all three blocks of gold clay, and roll it into a sheet ⅛" thick (#1 setting). Cut the rectangle in half, lay one half on top of the other, and use the brayer to roll the two sheets together. Trim the ¼" thick sheet into a 5" square. With the ruler, mark the center of the square. Cut a hole with the round cutter. Make sure the center of the clock motor fits through this hole. If not, widen the hole with a brush handle.

2 • Add the decorative edge

Mix ½ block of conditioned green clay with an equal amount of gold clay. Blend the two colors completely. Roll eight snakes of green-gold clay, ⅛" x 5". Take two of the snakes and gently twist them together. Repeat with the other snakes for a total of four twisted snakes. Squeeze a thin line of translucent liquid clay around the outside edge of the clock, ¼" from the edge. Lay the first snake parallel to the edge of the clock, and trim the end at a 45-degree angle, parallel to the diagonal of the clock. Trim the second twisted snake at a 45-degree angle, and match it up to the first snake, forming a mitered corner. Trim the second snake at an angle as you did the first, and repeat with the remaining snakes to complete the twisted edge on the clock.

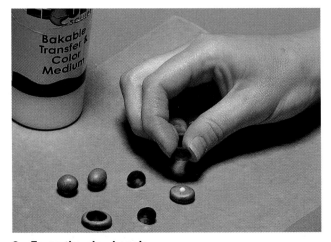

3 • Form the clay bezels

Roll four ⅝" balls of green-gold clay. Roll the balls into ovals, and then flatten them into discs about ¼" thick. On the first disk, put a dot of translucent liquid clay. Spread the clay into a thin layer, center the cabochon over the disk, and press the cabochon into the clay to form a bezel. Repeat for the other three cabochons.

4 • Attach the cabochons to the clock

Place a dot of translucent liquid clay on the clock base ¼" inside each corner formed by the twisted snakes. Align the first cabochon in the clay bezel diagonally with the corner of the clock, and press it onto the clock base, adhering it with the dot of clay. Repeat for the other three cabochons.

5 · Cut out the leaves

Roll the green-gold clay into a ⅛" thick sheet (#1 setting). Use the leaf cutter to cut nine leaf shapes.

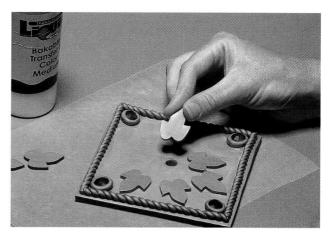

6 · Apply the leaves to the clock

Spread a thin coat of translucent liquid clay over the entire surface of the clock inside the decorative edge. Place all nine leaves on the face of the clock in a random arrangement. Press the leaves gently onto the base.

7 · Form the vines and stems

Roll six snakes ⅛" thick and 5" long. Form several scrolls at the ends of the snakes by rolling the ends carefully between your thumb and index finger. Place the scrolls and snakes onto the face of the clock between the leaves to form stems and vines. Trim the excess clay with a craft knife. When applying the vines, allow a ¼" clear space all the way around the center hole for the clock motor and hands, which will be inserted later. When all the vines are in place, bake the clock at 275 degrees (F) for 20 minutes. Allow the clock to cool.

8 · Put liquid clay on the leaves

Dot a small amount of translucent clay onto the surface of each leaf. Use your fingertip to spread the clay over the entire surface of each leaf.

9. Start to color the leaves

Place ½ teaspoon of translucent clay into each of two sections in a metal palette. To the first section, add a small dab (the size of a pin head) of red oil paint and an equal sized dab of black oil paint. To the same section, add 1/16 teaspoon of red-russet mica powder. Stir all the colors into the liquid clay completely to make deep burgundy tinted clay. In the second section, add ⅛ teaspoon of spring green mica powder, and stir it into the clay. With a skewer, place a few drops of burgundy liquid clay on one half of each leaf. Use the tip of the skewer to drag the clay to the edge of the leaves.

10 • Add green to the leaves

On the second half of each leaf, place a few drops of green tinted clay. Drag the color to the edge of each leaf.

11 • Add the details to the leaves

Place ½ teaspoon of translucent liquid clay in a third section of the metal palette. Add ⅛ teaspoon of pearl white mica powder and ¹⁄₁₆ teaspoon of gold iridescent glitter. Stir the powders into the clay. Pick up a small drop of pearl white clay on the pointed tip of a skewer. Place the tip of the skewer with the liquid clay at the center of the base of the first leaf. As the clay slides off the skewer, slowly move the skewer along the center of the leaf, creating a pearl white line dividing the green and burgundy clay. When you reach the tip of the leaf, lift the skewer, and wipe the tip of the skewer with a paper towel. Pick up a second drop of pearl white clay and place the skewer tip at the base of the leaf. This time, form a line down the center of the green half of the leaf. Repeat this step for the burgundy half of the leaf. Add pearl white to the other eight leaves.

12 • Feather the veins

To feather the veins on the leaves, start at the base of the center of the pearl white stripe on the first leaf. Using the pointed tip of the skewer, drag the point from the white into the burgundy clay, forming a fine diagonal stripe from the center to the edge of the leaf. Wipe the skewer with a paper towel before forming the next vein. Continue to drag the white clay from the center to the edge of the leaf at ⅛" intervals until you reach the tip of the leaf. Repeat the feathering on the other side of the center vein, dragging the white clay into the green. Once the center of the leaf is feathered, repeat the dragging steps for the side stripes of pearl white. Continue until all nine leaves are complete. Bake the clock at 275 degrees (F) for 10 minutes, and allow it to cool. **Note:** *As the clay is in a liquid form, make sure to work on a level surface.*

13 • Varnish the leaves and add the clock parts

Use a gloss varnish to finish only the surface of the leaves. When the varnish is dry, attach the clock movement and hands according to the manufacturer's directions. Install a battery in the clock, and set the time.

Fiorato Bead Necklace

MATERIALS&TOOLS

- 1 block translucent Premo
- 1 pinch of alizarin crimson Premo
- ½ block scrap clay
- 24 coordinating glass beads, 6mm
- 45 to 50 (one small vial) amber seed beads
- 10 small gold tone decorative bead caps
- 32 extra small gold tone decorative bead caps
- 20" Beadalon flexible wire cord, size .015
- 2 gold tone crimp beads
- 1 small gold tone lobster claw clasp

- 3 gold tone jump rings, ¼"
- 21 gold tone head pins, 2"
- Gold metallic leaf
- Basic tool kit (refer to page 17)
- Liquid polymer clay tool kit (refer to page 18)
- Baking kit (refer to page 17)
- White oil paint
- Pearl Ex mica pigment powders: brilliant gold, Aztec gold, antique gold, duo red-blue, red russet, true blue
- Fimo polymer clay varnish, gloss finish
- Flat brush, ½"

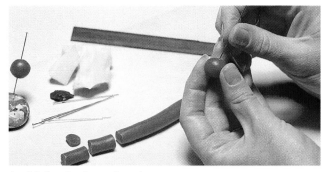

1 • Make the base beads

Condition the translucent Premo clay. To add color, mix in a small pinch of crimson clay. Add a little bit at a time to control the color, kneading the clay in your hands until the color is even. Roll the tinted clay into a ½" snake, cut one end flat, and then cut one ¾", two ½", and two ⅜" pieces from the snake. Roll each piece into a ball and pierce it through the center with a head pin. Do not slide the bead around; allow it to stick to the headpin (this will act as a handle later on). Stick the beads on headpins into a flattened ball of scrap clay (this will become your baking stand for the beads). Make sure the beads are not touching one another. Bake the beads in the stand for 15 minutes at 275 degrees (F).

2 • Make the extra clay beads

Roll the remaining clay snake down to a ⅜" diameter. Cover the snake with gold metallic leaf. Cut 16 pieces, ⅜" long, and roll them into balls. Pierce each ball through the center with a headpin, and press the headpins into a second flattened ball of scrap clay. Bake for 15 minutes at 275 degrees (F). Once cool, varnish the gold embellished beads and allow them to dry in the baking stand. Set the extra beads aside.

3 • Add aventurine to the beads

To create the aventurine color used on fiorato beads, place ½ teaspoon of translucent liquid clay in one section of the metal palette, and mix in ¹⁄₁₆ teaspoon each of antique gold and Aztec gold mica powders. The aventurine should have an almost paste-like texture. Add more powder if needed. Once your base beads have cooled, you can begin the decoration. Leave the headpins in the beads as handles. On the first bead, dip the fine brush in the aventurine and draw a line all the way around the bead. Dip the pointed end of a skewer into the aventurine clay and draw wavy lines around the bead above and below the centerline. (You may want to practice making lines on a sheet of wax paper.) If the liquid clay is runny, it can be set with a quick blast from a heat gun. Do not hold the heat gun too close to the bead, or you may flatten or scorch your liquid clay design. Repeat the aventurine designs on all five beads. Bake for 10 minutes at 275 degrees (F) in the baking stand. Allow the beads to cool. *Tip: The fiorato technique works best with thicker liquid clay. To thicken your tinted clay, set it aside in the metal palette, loosely covered for several days to weeks.*

4 • Make roses

Each bead has two roses applied on opposite sides of the bead along the centerline. To make the pink clay, in the palette mix ½ teaspoon of translucent liquid clay with ¹⁄₁₆ teaspoon duo red-blue mica powder. For the maroon, mix ¼ teaspoon of translucent liquid clay with ¹⁄₃₂ teaspoon of red-russet mica powder. For the white, use a dab (what fits on the end of the skewer) of white oil paint in ¼ teaspoon translucent liquid clay. Mix all the colors thoroughly; they should not be runny. To form the roses, use the end of a skewer to make a 3mm to 4mm dot of pink clay along the aventurine centerline of the bead. Dip the pointed end of the skewer into the maroon clay and place it into the center of the pink dot. Swirl the maroon clay through the pink clay, starting in the center and working out to the edge. Clean the skewer tip and repeat the motion using white clay. Set the rose with a heat gun. Repeat this procedure for the other side of the bead and on two sides for each of the other four beads.

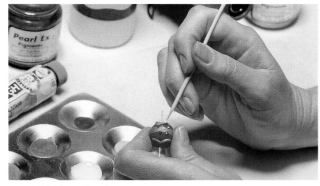

5 • Add blue flowers

Each bead has two blue flowers applied along the center aventurine line in the spaces where there are no roses. In one section of the palette, mix ¼ teaspoon translucent liquid clay with 1/32 teaspoon true blue mica powder. In another section, mix ¼ teaspoon liquid clay with 1/32 teaspoon brilliant gold mica powder for the yellow. In the space equidistant from each rose, make five dots of blue liquid clay in a small circle using the pointed tip of the skewer. After cleaning the skewer with a paper towel, dot white clay in the center of each blue dot. Complete the flower by making a yellow dot in the center of the circle of blue dots. The flower can be set with a heat gun. Repeat this step for the blue flower on the other side of the bead and on two sides of the other four beads. Bake all five beads in the baking stand for 15 minutes at 275 degrees (F).

6 • Varnish the beads

When the beads have cooled completely, varnish all five fiorato beads with the flat brush, and allow them to dry in the baking stand.

7 • Bead the necklace

Cut a 20" piece of Beadalon flexible wire cord. Start in the center of the necklace and thread the largest of the fiorato beads as the center. Thread a small bead cap on each side of the center bead followed by a seed bead next to each cap. The pattern for each side of the necklace is as follows: small cap, fiorato bead, small cap, seed bead, small cap, fiorato bead, small cap, seed bead, tiny cap, gold leaf clay bead, tiny cap, seed bead, glass bead, seed bead, tiny cap, gold leaf bead, tiny cap, seed bead, glass bead, seed bead, tiny cap, gold leaf bead, tiny cap, seed bead, glass bead, seed bead, tiny cap, gold leaf bead, tiny cap, seed bead, glass bead, seed bead, glass bead, seed bead, tiny cap, gold leaf bead, tiny cap, seed bead, glass bead, seed bead, glass bead, seed bead, tiny cap, gold leaf bead, tiny cap, seed bead, glass bead, seed bead, glass bead, seed bead, glass bead, seed bead, tiny cap, gold leaf bead, tiny cap, seed bead, glass bead, seed bead, glass bead, seed bead, tiny cap, gold leaf bead, tiny cap, seed bead, glass bead.

8 • Finish the necklace

Place a crimp bead at each end of the necklace and thread each end through a jump ring and back through the crimp bead. Tighten and crimp the crimp beads. Attach the clasp (refer to adding a clasp, page 42).

Fiorato Vase

- Glass vase
- Basic tool kit (refer to page 17)
- Liquid polymer clay tool kit (refer to page 18)
- Baking kit (refer to page 17)
- Oil paints: white, blue, sap green
- Pearl Ex mica pigment powders: Aztec gold, antique gold, duo red-blue, red russet, true blue, duo green-yellow, spring green
- Flat brush, ¼"
- Heat gun (not shown with materials)

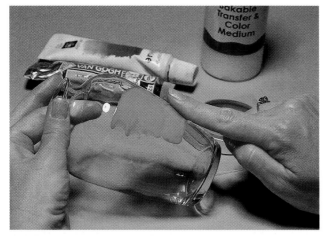

1 • Glaze the vase

In a small glass dish, mix 2 teaspoons of translucent liquid polymer clay with a small dab (one that fits on the end of a skewer) of blue oil paint and a small dab of sap green oil paint. Using a brush or your fingertip, paint the entire surface of the vase with tinted liquid clay. It is best to cover the entire vase at once to avoid seams in the glaze. Bake the vase standing up for 10 minutes at 275 degrees (F). Cool the glass vase slowly.

2 • Mix the aventurine color and add stripes

To create the aventurine color used for the fiorato look, place ½ teaspoon of translucent liquid clay in one section of the palette and mix in ¹⁄₁₆ teaspoon each of antique gold and Aztec gold mica powder. The aventurine should have an almost paste-like texture. Add more powder if needed. Once the vase has cooled, make a ³⁄₈" stripe of aventurine around the neck and a ½" stripe around the base of the vase. Also run a thin line around the lip of the vase. Bake the vase for 10 minutes at 275 degrees (F).

3 • Add aventurine embellishment

Once the vase has cooled, use the blunt end of a skewer to make a wavy line of aventurine over the aventurine stripes at the bottom and neck of the vase. This line can be set with a heat gun so that the vase does not have to be baked again right away. Be careful not to scorch or flatten the liquid clay design by holding the heat gun too close to the vase.

4 • Make blue and white dots

In one section of the metal palette, mix ½ teaspoon of translucent liquid clay with ¹⁄₁₆ teaspoon true blue mica powder. In another section, mix ½ teaspoon of translucent liquid clay with a dab (one that fits on the end of a skewer) of white oil paint. Using the skewer, make blue dots all the way around the lip of the vase. With the skewer tip, make tiny white dots in each blue dot. Set the dots with a heat gun. *Tip: The fiorato technique works best with thicker liquid clay. To thicken your tinted clay, set it aside in the metal palette, loosely covered for several days to weeks.*

5 • Add roses

In the metal palette, mix ½ teaspoon of translucent liquid clay with ¹⁄₁₆ teaspoon duo red-blue mica powder to make the pink clay. For the maroon, mix ½ teaspoon of liquid clay with ¹⁄₁₆ teaspoon red-russet powder. Mix both colors thoroughly; they should not be runny. To form a rose, make a 3 mm to 4 mm dot of pink clay with the flat end of a skewer in the dip of the wavy aventurine line on the neck of the vase. Place the pointed end of the skewer into the maroon clay and put it into the center of the pink dot. Swirl the maroon clay through the pink clay, starting in the center and working out to the edge. Clean the skewer tip and repeat the swirling motion using white clay. Continue to make roses all the way around the neck of the vase. Roses can be set as you go using a heat gun.

6 • Make the leaves

In one section of the metal palette, mix ½ teaspoon translucent liquid polymer clay with ¹⁄₁₆ teaspoon duo green-yellow mica powder to make a light green. In another section, mix ½ teaspoon of liquid clay with ¹⁄₁₆ teaspoon spring green mica powder to make a darker green. With a skewer, make light green dots in a triangular pattern around each rose. To form a leaf, draw a line through the center of each dot moving away from the rose using darker green clay. Leaves can be set with the heat gun. When all of the roses have leaves, bake the vase for 10 minutes at 275 degrees (F), and cool the vase slowly.

7 • Embellish the sides of the vase

Following the rose instructions in step 5, decorate the sides of the vase with randomly placed roses. Set the roses with a heat gun.

8 • Continue the vase embellishment

Following the leaf instructions in step 6, place two or three leaves around each rose. Set the leaves with a heat gun. Continue the embellishment by using a skewer to form wavy aventurine lines around the roses. Complete the decoration by making blue liquid clay dots in any empty spaces. Set each element with the heat gun as you go. Bake the vase for 10 minutes at 275 degrees (F). Cool the vase slowly.

9 • Complete the vase base

To complete the fiorato decoration of the vase, follow the instructions in steps 5 and 6, and make roses and leaves in each dip of the aventurine line at the base of the vase. At the crest of each wave, make a blue dot with a tiny white dot inside. Set each element with the heat gun as you go. Bake for 10 minutes at 275 degrees (F).

Gallery of Ideas

"Winds of Change." In this sculptural piece, the figure of the woman is placed into a marbled liquid polymer clay background that has been embellished with glass cabochons. The edges of her robes are gilded with liquid clay.

Clockwise from above:

1 Assorted fiorato beads and cabochons decorated with the classic rose pattern.

2 Fiorato-style decoration in liquid polymer clay on two vases, a votive, and beads. Once the technique has been mastered, different styles of decoration can emerge.

3 Fiorato beads and cabochons worked into completed pieces of jewelry. Some of these utilize bead shapes or patterns that may not appear in historical Italian glass bead work.

Chapter 9

Glass Effects

Adaptation of Techniques

Throughout history, glass has been used in works of art of many types and styles. Because of the nature of glass, glass pieces are often used to create colorful and unique patterns. Glass techniques offer a great source of inspiration to artists that work in other media as well.

Enamel

Enamel is defined as the application of an opaque or transparent colored, vitreous, glass-like coating fused onto a metal or glass base.[33] The earliest enamels were discovered on the island of Cyprus, an early producer of copper, and were dated from the thirteenth and eleventh centuries BC.[34] For the most part, enamels appear in two major techniques: champleve and cloisonné. Champleve is a technique in which recesses are formed in the metal by chasing, engraving, or casting, and then the recessed areas are filled with enamel. The enamel can then be polished so it is flush with the metal divisions.[35] In the fifteenth century, Limoges enamellers adopted a Venetian technique of painting enamel on glass. This enamel painting on metal did not require divisions or engraving, and it resembled contemporary enameling.[36]

Seventeenth century painted enamel portrait.

Cloisonné

Cloisonné is an enamel technique in which thin strips of metal are attached to a metal base to form compartments or "cloisons" into which the enamel is placed.[37] Oftentimes it requires multiple layers of glass and multiple firings for a piece to achieve its final look, where only the top edges of the metal strips are visible. Cloisonné dates back to the Egyptians in 4000 BC where they set semi-precious stones into gold filigree work. The cover of the coffin of Tutankhamen is a prime example. Cloisonné was evident in Greek work of the fifth century BC and in Byzantine work from the ninth to twelfth centuries AD.[38] The technique found its way to China around the thirteenth century AD where, in the hands of skilled craftsmen, it evolved into its own style.

Cloisonné has continued to be a valued traditional art in China. Even with the use of modern technology, Chinese cloisonné items are beautifully and elegantly embellished.[39]

Above: Chinese cloisonné horse and beads with contemporary cloisonné samples.
Right: Chinese cloisonné vase.

Stained Glass

Glass is a combination of quartz sand, soda, and lime. It was probably first discovered during the process of firing pottery. The Egyptians were using glass as early as 2700 BC. The origins of stained glass are not concretely documented, but the technique probably developed from jewelry making, cloisonné, and mosaic techniques.[40] Stained glass became known as the technique by which pieces of glass were cut and enclosed in strips of lead. Pieces were then soldered together. Stained glass flourished during the Gothic age with the construction of the great cathedrals in Europe. With the change in architecture came the need to fill larger openings in the cathedral walls. Gothic designers painted with glass, and stained glass became the leading form of illustration of the time.[41] During the Renaissance, the use of multicolored glass was dropped and window designers used white glass and then painted the designs on them. The Gothic revival of the late 1800s brought back the medieval stained glass techniques.[42]

John LaFarge and Louis Comfort Tiffany started experimenting with stained glass in America in the late 1800s. They developed the use of copper strips between the pieces of glass and are known for their fine cuts and flowing designs.[43] Stained glass as an art form has experienced a new revival over the past 30 years. The look and feel of stained glass can prompt techniques in other media such as polymer clay.

Stained glass window by Cristopher Lapp.

Glass Effects in Polymer Clay

The introduction of liquid polymer clay allows the polymer clay artist an opportunity to reproduce glasslike effects. Historical techniques such as enamel, cloisonné, and stained glass can be used for inspiration. The first two projects in this chapter imitate the look of enamel on metal. In the first project, the cuff, you will be forming your own metal backing for the liquid clay using metal foil. The foil will be embossed to form recesses for the liquid clay enamel. The cuff will be completed using metal findings, glass beads, and elastic cord. In the second project, the metal to be enameled is in the form of a button. The surfaces of the metal buttons are decorated with liquid clay. The enameled buttons are then used as decorative elements on a compact.

In the second section, the projects focus on cloisonné. The pin project is the simple application of creating foil wells and then filling them with liquid polymer clay. The second project, the cloisonné box, uses liquid clay to paint and decorate the sides of the box, and then the cloisonné lid is formed. The result is a beautiful and antique-looking keepsake.

In the third section of this chapter, there are two stained glass projects. The technique involves baking the project on glass so that the liquid clay forms very thin translucent sheets, reminiscent of glass. The earrings in the first project use glass cabochon embellishments. In this project, stained glass pieces are made in a small scale to use for jewelry applications. The second project is a holiday ornament. The larger scale stained glass effect can be used for window and tree ornaments, or it can be applied to glass objects such as vases.

Stained glass by Christine (Steen) V. Mitchell. In recent years, there has been a rise in stained glass as a hobby craft.

Enameled Cuff

MATERIALS & TOOLS

- ¾ block ultramarine Premo
- ¼ block gold Premo
- Patterns for enameled cuff, (page 138)
- ArtEmboss metal sheet (9 ¼" x 60" roll) lightweight aluminum craft foil, any color (you will use the silver back)
- 5 silver tone eye pins, 2"
- 6" clear beading elastic
- 5 sage green glass cube beads, 6mm
- 4 carnelian glass oval beads, 6mm

- Basic tool kit (refer to page 17)
- Liquid clay tool kit (refer to page 18)
- Baking kit (refer to page 17)
- Mica pigment powder: true blue, spring green, Aztec gold
- Embossing powder, clear with iridescent glitter
- Pointed wooden tool
- Old scissors or tin snips
- Fimo polymer clay varnish, gloss finish
- GS Hypo-Tube Cement

1 • Etch the bracelet pattern

Copy the pattern pieces (one center piece and two side pieces). With old scissors, cut one piece of craft foil, 2¼" x 3¼", and two pieces of craft foil, 2¼" x 3". Condition the ultramarine clay and roll it into a ⅛" thick sheet (#1 setting). Use the soft brush to dust the sheet lightly with cornstarch. Center the larger piece of craft foil with the colored side facing up over the sheet of clay. Center the pattern piece for the middle of the bracelet over the foil. Applying moderate pressure, use the pointed wooden tool to etch the pattern into the foil. Repeat this step for the two smaller pieces of foil, etching the pattern for the side sections of the bracelet into the foil.

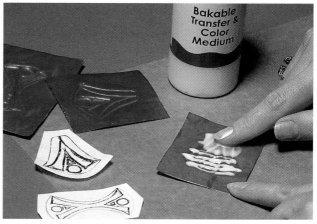

2 • Fill the etched pattern

Squeeze some translucent liquid clay onto the colored side of the large piece of foil. Use your fingertip to spread the clay and fill the etched grooves on the foil. Repeat the filling on the two smaller pieces of foil. Bake the three pieces of foil for 10 minutes at 275 degrees (F). Allow the foil to cool.

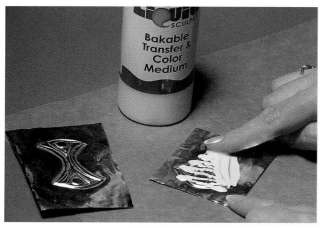

3 • Prepare foil for color

Spread a thin layer of translucent liquid clay over the silver side of all three pieces of foil.

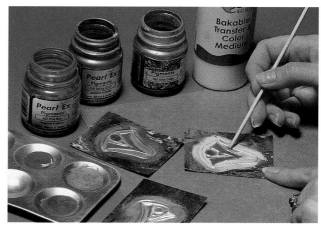

4 • Color the foil

In each of three sections on a metal palette, put ¼ teaspoon of translucent liquid clay. In the first section, add ¹⁄₁₆ teaspoon true blue mica powder. In the second section, add ¹⁄₁₆ teaspoon spring green mica powder. In the third section, add ¹⁄₁₆ teaspoon Aztec gold mica powder. Mix each of the colors thoroughly. Starting with a bracelet side piece, use the flat tip of the skewer to put a drop of green tinted clay in the two smallest shapes. Use the pointed tip to drag the color and cover the shape, without going over the etched lines. Use the same method to add a blue and then a gold outline. Repeat these coloring steps for the other two bracelet pieces.

5 • Add sparkle

When all three bracelet pieces are colored, sprinkle a layer of clear iridescent embossing powder over the surface of each piece of foil. Bake the three foil pieces for 10 minutes at 275 degrees (F). Allow the foil to cool.

6 • Add the clay backing

Cut out the foil bracelet shapes with old scissors, ⅛" beyond the etched outline edge. Condition the gold clay, and blend it completely with ultramarine clay to make a metallic green. Roll the clay into a ⅛" thick sheet (#1 setting). Use a brayer to flatten each foil piece. Place one foil piece onto the metallic green clay sheet, and cut around the foil shape, allowing a 1/16" edge of clay to extend beyond the foil. Repeat for the other two foil pieces.

7 • Add the clay trim

Roll the metallic green scraps into a 5/64" thick sheet (#3 setting). Cut seven ⅛" wide strips for the trim. Squeeze a thin line of liquid clay around the outer edge of each bracelet piece. On the first bracelet piece, press the clay trim, following the outline edge and sandwiching the foil. When you reach a corner, cut the trim at a 45-degree angle, mitering the corner with the next piece of trim. Continue all the way around the bracelet piece until all the raw edges of the foil are covered. Repeat for the other two bracelet pieces. Smooth the clay on the outside edge of the bracelet, making sure none of the foil edges stick out of the clay.

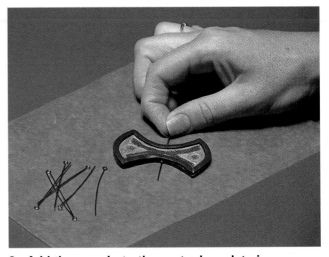

8 • Add the eye pin to the center bracelet piece

Carefully slide one eye pin through the clay layer at the narrowest section of the center bracelet piece. Slide the eye flush with the clay.

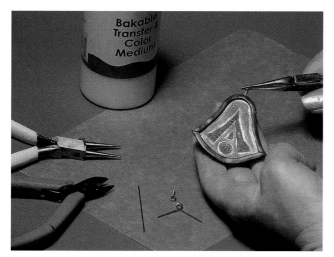

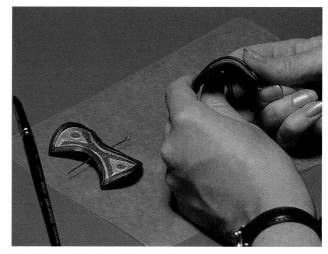

9 · Add loops to the side pieces

Use the round nose pliers to form a ⅛" loop in the center of an eye pin. Twist the ends together about four times below the loop. Trim the twisted end to ¼". Repeat the twisting for the other three eye pins. Holding a loop in the end of the pliers, dip it into a bit of translucent liquid clay. Carefully insert the loop into the middle of the wide curved end (in the clay layer) of a bracelet side piece until only the loop is sticking out. Place the second loop at the opposite narrow end of the bracelet side piece. Add the loops to the second bracelet piece.

10 · Curve the bracelet sections

When all loops have been added, curve the bracelet side pieces to fit the shape of your wrist. The foil will help the clay keep its shape. Bend the center bracelet section in the opposite direction than the side pieces. Bake all three bracelet pieces for 20 minutes at 275 degrees (F).

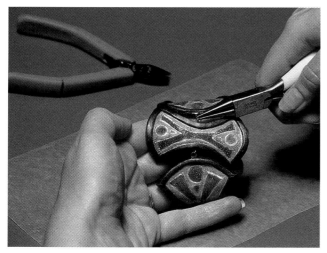

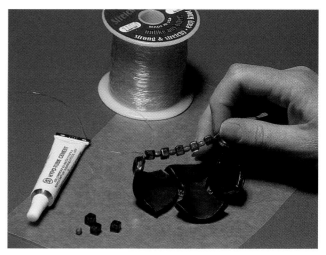

11 · Varnish and attach the pieces

When the bracelet pieces have cooled, varnish the surface of the foil and the clay trim, and allow the pieces to dry. Twist the eye pin in the center bracelet piece until it is perpendicular to the surface. Open the loop, hook it through the loop on one of the bracelet side pieces, and close the loop. On the opposite side, use your round nose pliers to form a loop, trim the excess wire, hook the loop through the second side bracelet piece, and close the loop. *Note: These loops may need to be secured more firmly with a bit of E-6000 industrial craft glue.*

12 · Add the beaded elastic closure

Knot the elastic three times onto one of the loops on the narrow end of a bracelet side piece. Start with a sage green cube bead, and string all nine beads onto the elastic, alternating colors with the carnelian oval beads. Knot the elastic three times on the second bracelet side piece, closing the bracelet. Place a dot of GS Hypo-Tube Cement on each elastic knot and allow the glue to dry before trimming the ends of the elastic. *Note: The size of the bracelet can be adjusted by the curve of the foil shapes and by adding or subtracting beads on the elastic.*

Enameled Button Compact

- 1 block black Premo
- Pattern for enameled button compact (page 139)
- Square mirror, 2" x 2"
- Sheer fabric (cotton or cotton blend), 2" x 3"
- 6 metal buttons
- 1 set Velcro self-adhesive squares
- Basic tool kit (refer to page 17)
- Liquid polymer clay tool kit (refer to page 18)
- Baking kit (refer to page 17)
- Purple oil paint
- Pearl Ex mica pigment powder:

Aztec gold, spring green
- Fimo polymer clay varnish, gloss finish
- Flat brush, ½"
- E-6000 industrial craft glue (not shown with materials)
- Metal ruler
- Brush cleaner

1 • Cut out the compact

Condition the black clay. Roll out a ⅛" thick sheet (#1 setting). Cut out one piece of clay using the pattern piece. Roll another sheet to a ⁵⁄₆₄" thickness (#3 setting), cut out two pieces of clay using the pattern piece as a guide. Roll out a ³⁄₆₄" thick sheet (#5 setting). Cut out one more piece of clay using the pattern piece.

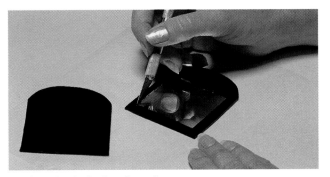

2 • Cut the hole for the mirror

Center the mirror ¼" from the flat hinge side of one of the ⁵⁄₆₄" thick (#3 setting) clay pattern pieces. Using a craft blade cut around the mirror.

3 • Make a fabric hinge

On a sheet of glass, spread a thin layer of translucent liquid clay smaller than 2" x 3". Lay the sheer piece of fabric into the clay and add extra liquid clay to the top of the fabric, spreading it gently with your fingers. Bake the fabric on the glass for 10 minutes at 265 degrees (F). Peel the fabric from the glass and trim it to 1" x 2⅜".

4 • Enamel buttons

In one section of the metal palette, mix ½ teaspoon of translucent liquid clay with ¹⁄₁₆ teaspoon of Aztec gold mica powder. In a second section, mix ½ teaspoon of translucent liquid clay with ¹⁄₁₆ teaspoon of spring green mica powder. In a third section, mix ½ teaspoon of translucent liquid clay with a dab (what fits on the end of a skewer) of purple oil paint. Using a skewer, decorate each of the six metal buttons with a series of dots of colored liquid clay. **Note:** *If you use buttons with indentations, the liquid clay can be used to fill those holes with color.* Bake the buttons for 10 minutes at 275 degrees (F), cool, and cut off the shanks with wire clippers.

5 • Place the buttons

On one side of the ⅛" thick (#1 setting) clay pattern piece, arrange the buttons to your liking, and press each one lightly into the clay to leave a shank indentation. Remove the buttons; they will be glued in later.

6 · Add a hinge

Brush a line of translucent liquid clay ⅜" wide on the hinge end of the ¾4" thick (#5 setting) clay pattern piece. Lay ⅜" of one end of the fabric hinge over the liquid clay. Brush more liquid clay over the entire piece, including the fabric, and lay the ⅛" thick clay pattern piece (right side up) over the ¾4" thick piece. The fabric should be sandwiched between the two pieces of clay. Press on the top clay pattern piece gently to eliminate any air pockets. Bake the clay flat for 15 minutes at 275 degrees (F). Cool it flat.

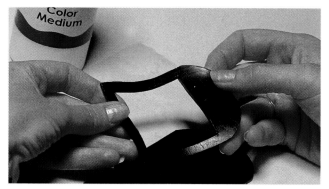

7 · Complete the hinge

Brush a line of translucent liquid clay ⅜" wide on the ⁵⁄₆4" thick (#3 setting) clay pattern piece that does not have the mirror hole in it. Lay the side of the fabric hinge not attached to the other pattern pieces over the liquid clay. Brush the entire piece with more liquid clay. Lay the piece with the mirror hole over the fabric, sandwiching the other side of the hinge between both pieces of clay.

8 · Attach the mirror

Place the mirror into the square hole on the unbaked side of the compact. Press the clay around it so that it fits snugly. Bake the compact flat for 15 minutes at 265 degrees (F). Cool flat.

9 · Attach Velcro

Once the compact has cooled, lift the mirror back out and glue it in place using E-6000 industrial craft glue. The edges of the compact can be trimmed and sanded if you wish. On the inside of the compact on the rounded ends, peel the backing from the adhesive on the loop piece of Velcro and press it in place next to the mirror. Attach the hook piece of Velcro on the inside of the compact cover.

10 · Attach the buttons

On the compact cover, glue on the buttons, matching them up to the shank indentations.

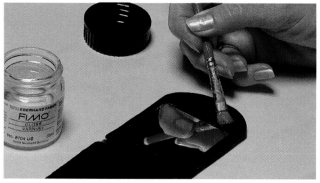

11 · Varnish the compact

Use the flat brush to varnish the inside and outside of the compact with Fimo polymer clay gloss varnish. Allow the varnish to dry completely.

Cloisonné Pin

MATERIALS &TOOLS

- ¼ block Premo: silver, violet
- Pattern for cloisonné brooch (page 139)
- ArtEmboss metal sheet lightweight aluminum craft foil (you will use the silver back), 9¼" x 60" roll
- Flat back glass or crystal rhinestones, assorted sizes
- Pin back, 1½"
- Basic tool kit (refer to page 17)
- Liquid polymer clay tool kit (refer to page 18)
- Baking kit (refer to page 17)

- Pearl Ex mica pigment powders: bright yellow, duo red-blue, spring green
- Ultramarine violet oil paint
- Old scissors or tin snips
- Pointed wooden stick or old ball point pen (no ink)
- Fimo polymer clay varnish, gloss finish
- Flat brush, ½"
- Brush cleaner

1 • Make the sheet for the pin base
Condition the silver and violet clays, and mix them together completely. Roll the silver-violet clay into a ⅛" thick square sheet (#1 setting). Place the pin pattern on top of the clay. Etch the pattern onto the clay by applying light pressure with the pointed wooden stick while following the lines on the pin pattern photocopy.

2 • Prepare the foil strips
With old scissors, cut four strips of craft foil, ½" x 9¼". Use a table edge to fold the foil strips in half lengthwise. Flatten the folded foil strips using the side of the wooden stick. Trim the foil strips to a width of ⅛".

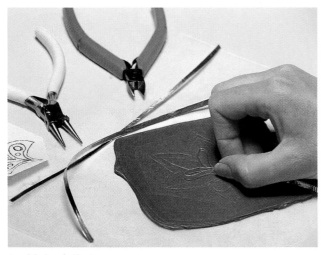

3 • Make foil shapes
Using the paper pattern as a guide, bend the foil strips with the round nose pliers to match the scroll designs on the pin pattern. Trim the shapes to size with the wire clippers.

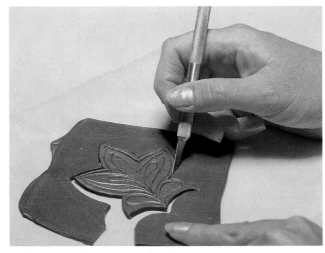

4 • Putting shapes into the clay:
Press the foil shapes into the etched clay, fold side up (the raw edges of the foil should be pressed into the clay). Using the paper pattern as a guide, form the foil shapes for the outside edge of the pin. Press the foil-edge shapes into the clay. When all the foil elements are in the clay, trim the outer edge of the pin with a craft knife ⅛" from the foil outline. Bake the pin at 275 degrees (F) for 20 minutes. Allow the pin to cool. **Note:** *Since the foil strips form the wells for the liquid clay to create the cloisonné effect, it is important to make closed shapes, or the clay will spread into other areas on the pin.*

5 • Mix the tinted clay and start to color the pin

In a metal palette, squeeze ½ teaspoon of translucent liquid clay into each of four sections. In the first section, scoop ⅛ teaspoon of bright yellow pigment powder into the liquid clay. Mix the color in completely. Make sure to wipe the skewer with a paper towel each time you mix a new color. In the second section, add ⅛ teaspoon of duo red-blue into the liquid clay and mix. In the third section, mix in ⅛ teaspoon of spring green mica powder. In the fourth section, add a dab (the size of half of a pea) of ultramarine violet oil paint. Mix thoroughly. Use the dull end of the skewer to place a few drops of yellow tinted liquid clay into the outside edge of the pin defined by the foil. Use the pointed end of the skewer to drag the color into the smaller areas of the foil barriers. Use the same method to add violet liquid clay into the center shapes. Bake the pin at 275(F) degrees for 10 minutes, and allow it to cool.

6 • Add more color

Using the skewer, fill the center section with duo red-blue tinted clay. Fill the bottom two sections with green liquid clay, once again dragging the clay to the edges of the foil wells.

7 • Place the stones and finish the pin

Press a pinch of the scrap clay onto the pointed tip of the skewer. This will form a tool for placing the rhinestones. Pick up a stone with the clay tip on the skewer, and place the stone in the desired spot on the pin. Drop it carefully into the unbaked liquid clay backing, not moving the stone around. Add all the stones. Bake the pin again for 10 minutes at 275 degrees (F), and allow it to cool. Apply the pin back (refer to Attaching pin backs, page 22). If the pin back is placed vertically from the upper tip of the pin, it can be hooked over a chain and worn as a pendant as well as a pin. Varnish the pin and allow it to dry.

Cloisonné Treasure Box

MATERIALS & TOOLS

- 1 block Premo: medium red brilliant, gold
- Pattern for cloisonné treasure box (page 139)
- Wooden box with hinged lid, 3½" wide x 5½" long x 3" deep
- 4 purple flat back glass cabochons, 10 mm
- 1 orange faceted flat back glass cabochon, 13 mm
- 1 purple ArtEmboss metal sheet lightweight aluminum craft foil, 9¼" x 60" roll
- Basic tool kit (refer to page 17)
- Liquid polymer clay tool kit (refer to page 18)
- Baking kit (refer to page 17)
- Pearl Ex mica pigment powders:

duo red-blue, red-russet, sparkle gold, sparkle copper
- Oil paints: ultramarine violet, sap green
- Glitter (very fine, heat resistant): copper, orange
- Gildenglitz variegated metallic leaf flakes
- Pointed wooden tool
- Old scissors or tin snips
- Fimo polymer clay varnish, gloss finish
- Flat brush, ½"
- Old brush with stiff bristles, ¾"
- Brush cleaner
- Optional: medium grit sandpaper
- Paper crimper

1 • Paint the first layer on the box

Prepare the wood box for liquid clay application (refer to Materials preparation, page 44). In a small glass dish, squeeze 3 tablespoons of translucent liquid clay. Add ½ teaspoon of red-russet mica powder. Stir in the powder thoroughly. Use the stiff brush to paint a thin coat of red-russet tinted liquid clay over the outside surface of the box (including the bottom), except for the center of the lid. Wipe the excess off the hinges, keeping the box closed. Place the box upside down on a baking tray lined with wax paper. Bake for 10 minutes at 265 (F) degrees. Allow the box to cool. Paint the inside of the box with red-russet liquid clay. Wipe the excess off the lip where the box closes and off the inside of the hinges. Bake the box with the lid open for 10 minutes, and then cool. Clean the brush thoroughly with isopropyl alcohol and a paper towel.

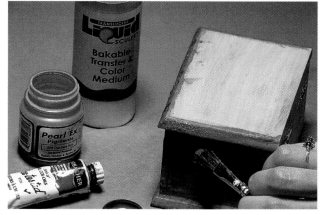

2 • Stipple the box

In a second small glass dish, squeeze 3 tablespoons of translucent liquid clay. Add a pea-size dab of ultramarine violet oil paint to make a medium purple shade. Add ¼ teaspoon of duo red-blue mica powder, and mix it thoroughly with the skewer. Using the stiff bristle tips of the brush, stipple a layer of purple liquid clay over the red-russet base coat. Cover the outside of the box, wiping the excess from the hinges.

3 • Add metallic accents

With the tip of your finger, dab on small metal leaf flakes randomly over the surface, covering part of the stippled clay. Burnish flakes onto the box so they are flat. Stipple clay lightly over the metallic areas. Bake the box for another 10 minutes at 265 degrees (F). When the box has cooled, stipple the inside, avoiding the lip of the box. Bake the box again for 10 minutes, and cool. It is not necessary to apply the metallic leaf to the inside. You may notice some bubbling of the liquid clay as it bakes onto the wood. This enhances the texture of the finished box.

4 • Create the clay lid base

Condition the red and gold clays, and mix the two colors together completely. When you have achieved a rich even metallic orange color, roll the clay into a ⅛" thick sheet (#1 setting). With the metal ruler and a craft knife, trim the sheet to fit the lid of your box (3¼" x 5"). Cut out the box lid pattern, and center it over the orange clay sheet. Use the pointed wooden tool to etch the box lid pattern onto the clay, and remove the pattern.

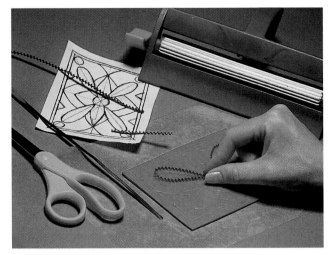

5 • Prepare foil strips

With the old scissors, cut ten strips of craft foil, ½" x 9¼". Use a table edge to fold the foil strips in half lengthwise. Flatten the folded foil strips using the side of the wooden stick. Trim the foil strips to a width of ⅛". Run three strips through the paper crimper. Leave the others flat.

6 • Shaping the foil strips

Using the paper pattern as a guide, bend the foil strips with the round nose pliers to match the scroll designs on the box pattern. Trim the shapes to size with the wire clippers. Press the foil shapes into the etched clay, fold side up; the raw edges of the foil should be pressed into the clay. Start from the center of the design and work outwards. **Note:** *Since the foil strips form the wells for the liquid clay to create the cloisonné effect, it is important to make closed shapes, or the clay will spread into other areas on the box lid.*

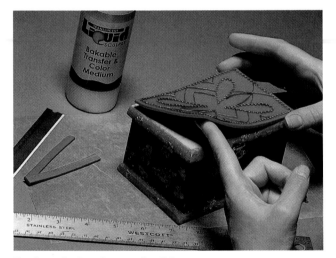

7 • Attach the clay to the lid

When all the foil strips have been pressed into the clay, gently roll a brayer over the surface of the strips to level them out. Spread a thin coat of translucent clay onto the lid of the box. Place the orange clay sheet with the foil pattern onto the lid of the box, centering the sheet of clay, and press the clay carefully onto the lid. Trim the clay edge if necessary.

8 • Form clay bezels for the stones

Using scraps of orange clay, roll one ball ⅜" in diameter and four balls ¼" in diameter. On a piece of wax paper, press each ball into a ¼" thick disk. Spread a thin layer of translucent liquid clay on the surface of each disk. Press the orange stone into the center of the largest disk, sinking it into the clay slightly. Press each of the four purple stones into the remaining four disks. Place a dot of translucent liquid clay into the center of the foil pattern on the box lid. Peel the orange stone in the clay bezel off the wax paper, and press it onto the center of the lid. Place a dot of translucent liquid clay in each of the four corners, ¼" inside the crimped foil edge. Press each of the purple stones into one corner of the box, inside the foil barrier. Bake the entire box and the lid at 265 degrees (F) for 20 minutes. Allow the box to cool.

9 • Start adding color to the lid

In one section of a metal palette, place ½ teaspoon translucent liquid clay. With the tip of the skewer, add a small dab (the size of a pin head) of sap green oil paint and ¹⁄₁₆ teaspoon of sparkle gold mica powder. Stir in the colors completely (you will use this color later). In a second section, add ¹⁄₁₆ teaspoon of sparkle copper mica powder along with ¹⁄₁₆ teaspoon each of copper and orange glitter. Stir in the colors to make sparkling copper liquid clay. With the flat tip of a skewer, place a few drops of copper glitter clay in each of the four foil wells surrounding the center orange stone. Use the tip of the skewer to drag the color to fill the wells completely. Wipe your skewer with a paper towel between colors. Add the red-russet clay (the same color used to tint the box) to each of the eight foil wells surrounding the purple stones. Drag the color to fill each well completely. After you have added the copper and red-russet colors, bake the box for 10 minutes at 265 degrees (F), and allow it to cool.

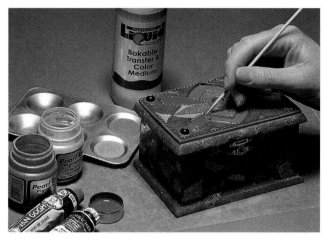

10 • Add green and purple accents:

Use the flat end of the skewer to place several drops of medium purple clay (which you mixed for the exterior of the box) in each of the four elongated foil shapes near the center of the lid, and drag the color to the edges. Add the green-gold clay to the remaining sections and drag the color to fill the foil shapes. When all the foil shapes have been filled, bake the box for 10 minutes at 265 degrees (F).

11 • Varnish the box

When all the colors have been added and baked, varnish the box with a gloss finish polymer clay varnish. It is best to do this in stages. Varnish the inside first, and leave it open as it dries. Next varnish the sides and bottom, and allow them to dry while the box rests on its lid. Finally, varnish the lid, including the glass stones. Allow the box to dry completely.

Stained Glass Drop Earrings

MATERIALS & TOOLS

- ¼ block Premo: black, silver
- 4 amber faceted flat back glass stones, 9mm
- 2 earring posts
- 2 earring nuts
- 2 gold tone head pins, ⅞"
- 2 gold tone 2" eye pins or two pieces of 20 gauge wire
- Basic tool kit (refer to page 17)
- Liquid polymer clay tool kit (refer to page 18)
- Baking kit (refer to page 17)
- Oil paints: red, yellow

- Fimo polymer clay varnish, gloss finish
- Very fine pointed brush
- Brush cleaner
- Round cutter, ½"

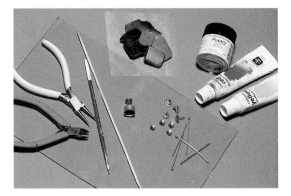

1 · Make the stone bezels

Condition the silver and black clays, and mix them together completely to make a dark metallic gray. Roll four balls of gray clay, each ¼" in diameter. On a piece of wax paper, press each ball into a ⅛" thick disk. Spread a thin layer of translucent liquid clay on the surface of each disc. Press an amber glass stone into the center of each disc, sinking the stone in slightly. On the piece of glass, spread a thin layer of translucent liquid clay in a 1" circle. About 3" from the first circle, make another thin 1" circle of liquid clay. Spread two thin 2" x 3" ovals of translucent liquid clay 1" below each of the two circles. Place the first two amber stones into the center of each of the translucent circles of clay on the glass. Press an amber glass stone into the center of each oval of translucent clay.

2 · Form the decorative edge for the earring tops

Roll two snakes of gray metallic clay to ⅟₁₆" x 2". Wrap the first snake around the outer edge of one amber stone in the clay bezel to form a thin decorative edge. Where the snake meets, pinch the ends together to form a teardrop, and trim the excess clay with a craft knife. Add the snake around the second stone and trim, same as the first.

3 · Add head pins

Starting at the end of the stone setting opposite the tear drop point, use the pliers to slide a head pin through the center of the clay bezel. The pointed end of the head pin should come out of the clay at the point of the teardrop. Push the head of the pin so it is flush with the snake edge. Repeat for the second stone setting.

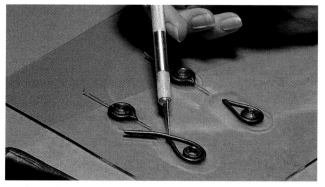

4 · Start forming the earring drops

Roll two snakes of gray clay, ⅟₁₆" x 3". Wrap the first snake around one of the amber stones on the glass (see picture). Pull the ends of the snake into a teardrop shape, leaving a ³⁄₁₆" gap between the clay bezel and the place where the snake meets to form the point of the teardrop. The teardrop should be about ¾" long. Trim the ends of the teardrop with the craft knife. Form the second earring drop with the other snake, and trim the excess clay.

5 · Enhance the earring drops

Roll two more dark gray clay snakes, ⅟₁₆" x 4". On the first earring drop, use one snake to form another larger teardrop outlining the first one. The gap between the bottom of the first teardrop and the second should be about ¼". The larger teardrop should be about 1¼" long. Trim the snake at the top of the teardrop with the craft knife.

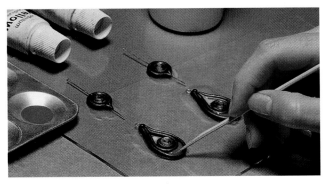

6 • Add loops for drops

Use the round nose pliers to form a ⅛" loop in the center of a head pin or piece of wire. Twist the ends together about four times below the loop. Trim the twisted end to ¼". Holding the loop in the end of the pliers, carefully insert the twisted section below the loop into the top of the teardrop. Press it all the way in until only the loop is sticking out of the clay. The loop should be parallel to the surface of the glass. Roll a ¹⁄₁₆" ball of clay and stick it at the top of the teardrop just below the loop. Repeat the loop application steps for the second earring drop. When the drops are complete, bake the earrings on the glass for 15 minutes at 275 degrees (F). Allow the glass and the earrings to cool completely. Leave the earring drops attached to the glass.

7 • Mix the stained glass colors

In one section of the metal palette, squeeze ½ teaspoon of translucent liquid clay. With the tip of the skewer, add a dab (the size of half of a pea) of red oil paint, and mix it in completely to make strong red tinted liquid clay. Wipe the skewer with a paper towel. In the second section of the metal palette, squeeze ½ teaspoon of translucent liquid Sculpey. Add a dab (the size of half a pea) of yellow oil paint and mix. Squeeze a small drop of translucent clay into each opening (there are four) in the two earring drops. With the pointed tip of the skewer, put a drop of yellow clay above the amber stone on each earring drop. Swirl the yellow and translucent clays together. Make sure the liquid clay fills the opening entirely. Wipe the excess liquid clay off the top of the snakes with your finger. Place two drops of red-tinted clay in the opening at the bottom of the teardrop. Blend the red and translucent liquid clays together completely, filling the opening. When both the red and the yellow areas are filled and blended on both earring drops, bake the earrings on the glass for 10 minutes at 275 degrees (F). Allow the glass and earrings to cool.

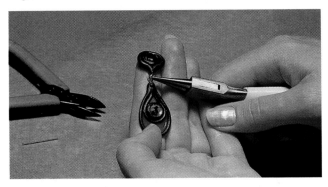

8 • Varnish the earrings

Remove the earring drops from the cool glass by cutting around the edge with a craft knife. Varnish only the red and yellow sections of the earring drops with a very small brush. Do not varnish the clay snakes. Allow the varnish to dry.

9 • Attach the earring drops

Use the pliers to form a loop at the bottom of the earring top. Bend the wire carefully so as not to crack the thin clay. The loop should be perpendicular to the top. Trim the wire, hook the loop from the earring top through the loop on the earring drop, and close the loop on the top. The drop should face forward. Repeat for the second earring.

10 • Attach the earring posts

Use your gray clay scraps to attach earring posts to the earrings (refer to Attaching earring posts, page 23).

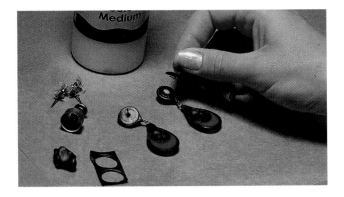

Stained Glass Holly Ornament

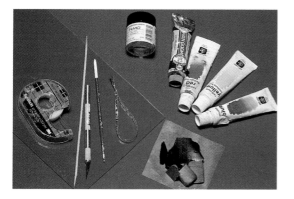

MATERIALS & TOOLS

- ½ of a block Premo: black, silver
- Pattern for stained glass holly ornament (page 139)
- 10" gold ribbon, 1/4" wide
- Basic tool kit (refer to page 17)
- Liquid polymer clay tool kit (refer to page 18)
- Baking kit (refer to page 17)
- Oil paint: red, sap green, blue, yellow
- Fimo polymer clay varnish, gloss finish
- Very fine pointed brush
- Brush cleaner
- Tape (clear or masking)

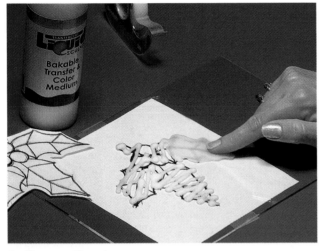

1 • Prepare the glass

Tape the ornament pattern to the backside of the glass. Spread a thin layer of liquid clay onto the surface of the glass, covering the holly design.

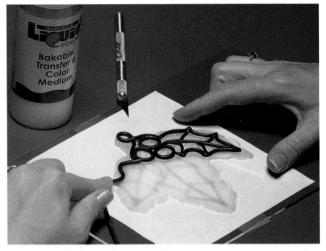

2 • Form the ornament outline

Condition the silver and black clays, and mix them together until they are blended completely into a dark metallic gray. Roll 10 snakes of gray clay ⅛" thick and 6" long. Start to place the snakes on the glass, following the lines on the ornament pattern. Use the craft knife to shape and trim the snakes to fit the pattern. Make sure all snakes form closed shapes and connect to each other. Use a snake to form the hanging loop at the top of the ornament. Connect the loop to the ornament. Remove the pattern from the back of the glass. Bake the ornament on the glass at 275 degrees (F) for 15 minutes. Allow the ornament and the glass to cool. Leave the ornament attached to the glass.

3 • Prepare the ornament for color

Squeeze and a few drops of translucent liquid clay into each well formed by the clay 'lead' snakes.

4 • Tint the berries

In the first section of the metal palette, squeeze ½ teaspoon of translucent liquid clay. With the tip of the skewer, add a dab (the size of half of a pea) of red oil paint, and mix it into the clay completely. With the skewer, drop several drops of red tinted liquid clay into each berry shape. Swirl the red and translucent clays until they are blended and fill the shapes.

5 · Tint the leaves

In the second section of the palette, squeeze ½ teaspoon of translucent liquid clay, and mix a small dab (the size of a pin head) of blue and an equal amount of yellow oil paint into the liquid clay to make a dark green. In the third section in the palette, squeeze ½ teaspoon of translucent liquid clay. Add a dot (just what fits on the flat tip of a skewer) of sap green oil paint to mix a light green. With the tip of a skewer, put a few drops of light green clay into each section on one side of each leaf. Blend the green and translucent clay, and fill each section. Add the dark green to the other side of each leaf, and fill each shape completely. Use your finger to wipe the excess clay off the surface of the clay snakes. When all the wells are filled with colored clay and blended, bake the ornament on the glass for 10 minutes at 275 degrees (F). Allow the glass and the ornament to cool.

6 · Varnish the ornament

Use the craft knife to cut around the edge of the ornament to remove it from the glass. Cut the translucent film out of the hanging loop. Use a very small brush to varnish only the colored translucent clay to create the stained glass effect. Wipe any varnish off the clay snakes. Allow the varnish to dry. Pull the narrow gold ribbon through the clay loop, and tie the ends together to make a loop in the ribbon so the ornament is ready for hanging.

Gallery of Ideas

Section 1 • Enamel

Left: Molded solid polymer clay pin enhanced with liquid clay 'enamel.'

Above: Multi-technique floral necklace. Leaves have been enameled with liquid polymer clay and embellished with glass cabochons.

Section 2 • Cloisonné

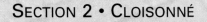

Above: Cloisonné mirror frame, box, and jewelry. Metal foil was used to construct the 'cloisons' on all of the pieces. The sections were then filled with one or more colors of tinted liquid clay.

Right: Cloisonné picture frame, memory book, and box.

Clockwise from above:

1 Stained glass effect applied to a glass vase or made into a sun catcher. Note the marbled effect of the liquid clay in the sections that imitate multicolored glass.

2 Stained glass effect applied to necklace construction. The stained glass sections are embellished with glass cabochons.

3 Variety of stained glass ornaments. On two of these ornaments, more than one color of tinted liquid clay was used to give the glasswork more depth.

Patterns and Transfers

Project #1: Transfer Cameo Pendant

Transfer for pendant: *Classic Clip Art* (New York: Glorya Hale Books, Random House Value Publishing, Inc., 1996) page 116.

Project #3: Clay Fabric Choker

Transfer for clay fabric choker: *700 Victorian Ornamental Designs* (New York: Dover Publications, Inc., 1998) plate 89.

Project #2: Transfer Window Candle Lamp

Transfer for candle lamp: *700 Victorian Ornamental Designs* (New York: Dover Publications, Inc., 1998) plate 4.

Pattern for candle lamp

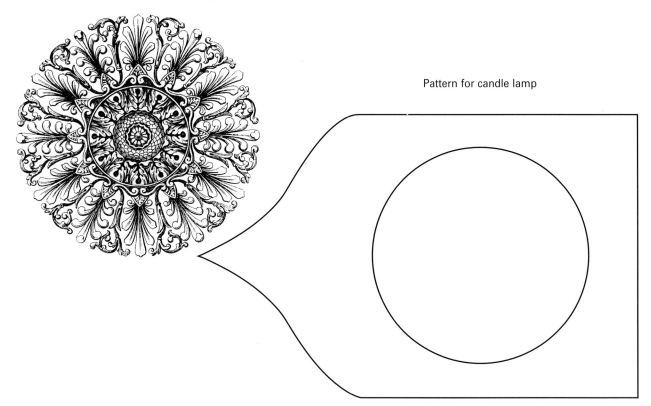

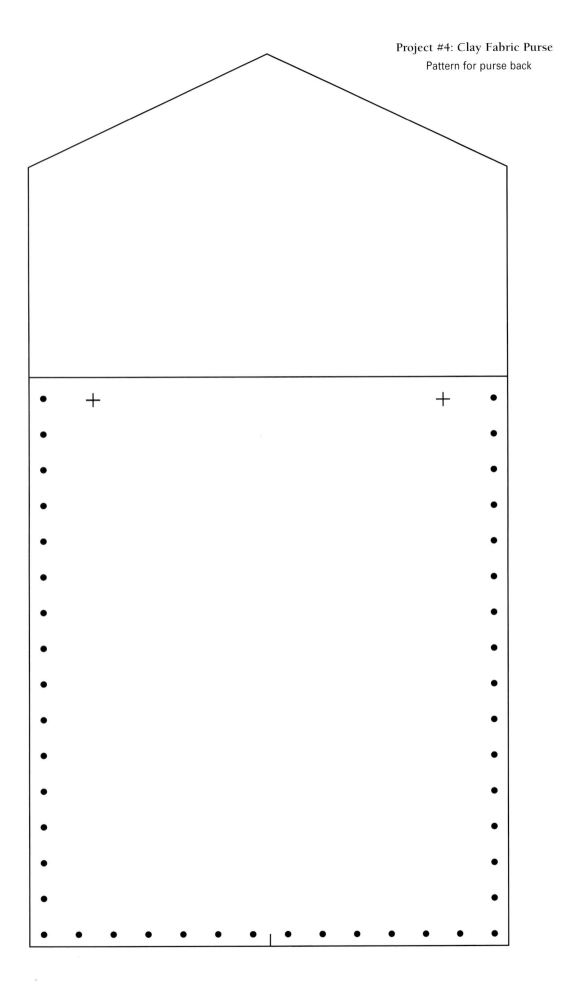

Project #4: Clay Fabric Purse

Pattern for purse front

Transfer for clay fabric purse: *700 Victorian Ornamental Designs* (New York: Dover Publications, Inc., 1998) plate 94.

Project #7: Shell Necklace
Pattern for shell necklace drop

Project #12: Terra Cotta Picture Frame
Transfer for carved tile on frame: *Floral Ornament* (New York: Dover Publications, Inc., 1997) p. 28.

Project #5: Grape Leaf Textured Barrette
Pattern for textured barrette

Project #17: Enameled Cuff
Patterns for enameled cuff, center, and side

Project #18: Enameled Button Compact
Pattern for enameled button compact

Project #20: Cloisonné Treasure Box
Pattern for cloisonné treasure box

**Project #22: Stained Glass
Holly Ornament**
Pattern for stained glass
holly ornament

Project #19: Pin
Pattern for cloisonné
brooch

Glossary

Aventurine—a chestnut-colored glass with copper-gold flecks.

Barrette—a clasp designed for holding hair. "Made in France" barrettes are of a superior quality.

Bezel—a rim or setting for holding a stone in place.

Brayer—a small roller with a handle. Acrylic works best for polymer clay.

Burnish—to smooth a surface by rubbing with a flat tool, refers to applying metallic leaf or transfer images to clay.

Cabochon—convex round or oval stone, usually not faceted. In this book, it is used as a general term for a stone applied to a project.

Cane—thin rods of colored glass stacked to form an intricate pattern that runs lenghtwise through the stack. The term can be applied to solid polymer clay as well.

Clay fabric—a cotton, cotton blend, or other type of fabric (preferably sheer) that has been infused with liquid polymer clay and baked in order to create a clay fabric to be used for flexible clay elements in polymer clay and mixed media applications.

Cloisonné—enamel work in glass on metal where the colors are separated by thin metal bands.

Conditioning—softening and working polymer clay until it is malleable and ready for use.

Craft foil—medium weight ArtEmboss craft foil. It is colored on one side and silver on the other, lightweight enough to shape and emboss easily, and heavy enough to retain its shape (heavier than kitchen foil).

Decoupage—the method of decorating an object with paper cutouts.

Diluent—made by Polyform Products, it is a liquid used to soften solid polymer clay and to thin liquid polymer clay.

E bead—a larger size glass seed bead, usually 3mm to 4mm.

Earring nuts—available in several styles, the earring nuts are the components that slide onto the post of an earring to secure them to the ear.

Earring post—a thin piece of wire with a flat pad soldered to one end. The wire is the part of the post that goes through the ear, and the pad is attached to the back of the ornament that decorates the ear.

Enamel—glass or a glassy substance fused to the surface of metal or other materials for decorative purposes.

Eye pin—a piece of wire with a loop on one end, generally used to attach beads together in a linked fashion.

Eyelet—a metal ring for lining a small hole that is there for the passage of cording for a strap or lacing.

Fiorato—a type of Italian lampworked glass bead embellished with flowers and scrolls created by molten glass.

Flat back—a cabochon or rhinestone with a flat back. Flat back stones are good for attaching to flat surfaces when there is no bezel to support the stone.

Foil back—a metallic coating often applied to the back of flat and faceted rhinestones and glass cabochons to enhance their shine and color. Special glue is often needed to apply foil-backed stones.

Gauge—a standard of measurement used to define the thickness of wire.

Glaze—an applied surface coating. When used in reference to polymer clay, it can be either glossy or matte.

Glitter—small particles of a metallic material that add sparkle when applied to a surface.

Head pin—a wire with a small flat head attached on one end, usually used for making beaded drops in jewelry making.

Impression—a pattern formed by pressing a stamp or object into clay or other malleable materials.

Impression glazing—using tinted liquid clay to fill and glaze the impressions made by a stamp or another object in solid polymer clay.

Jewelry findings—a general term used to refer to many types of parts such as pin backs, jump rings, earring posts, and other parts used in jewelry making.

Jump ring—a single loop of wire forming a ring with a small gap on one side that is easily manipulated to connect parts in jewelry making.

Lampwork—glass bead making in which molten glass rods or tubes are formed into beads with the aid of a small flame.

Marbling—the process of coloring or staining a surface to imitate variegated marble. For liquid polymer clay, it refers to dragging several colors of liquid clay across the surface of a project to create decorative patterns.

Metallic leaf—a composition metal sheet that is tissue thin and can be applied to clay or other surfaces.

Mica pigment powder—a fine powder of mica particles often used to add a pearlescent sheen to both solid and liquid polymer clay, available in a wide range of colors.

Millefiore—an Italian term meaning 'thousand flowers' applied to glass beads and objects covered with fine canes that form intricate patterns. It is also applied to a polymer clay technique for layering colors to create complex canes.

Mokume Gane—a term borrowed from a type of Japanese metalsmithing, also used to refer to a solid polymer clay technique of layering, texturing, and cutting thin slices of clay to create a wood grain effect.

Mold—a hollow form used to give a shape or dimensional form to a material.

Mosaic—a picture or pattern created with many pieces and elements of glass, ceramic, stone, or a variety of other materials.

Needle nose pliers—hand held pincers with long narrow tips that are flat on the inside edge; often used for bending wire in jewelry making.

Oil-based pencils—colored pencils for artwork that cannot be blended with water. The oil base in these colors works well with photocopy transfers on polymer clay.

Oil paint—an artist's paint that is most often made by adding powdered pigment to an oil base, usually linseed oil (oil paint is very effective for tinting liquid polymer clay).

Pasta machine—a metal rolling machine that is either hand cranked or powered by a motor. Developed for making sheets of pasta, it is easily adapted to solid polymer clay for making uniform sheets (once it is used for clay, it should not be used again for food).

Plasticizer—a substance added to polymer clay in order to make it softer, more flexible, or viscous.

Reverse mold—a form or relief made from an existing mold that, when hardened, can then be used as a mold to make a form resembling the original object.

Rhinestone—a sparkling faceted stone usually composed of crystal with either a faceted or flat back.

Round nose pliers—small hand-held pincers with long tips that are rounded on the ends, most often used in forming wire loops or spirals in jewelry making.

Saturate—the action of allowing unbaked liquid polymer clay to soak through a piece of fabric until it is visible on the other side of the fabric, leaving a slightly shiny surface (applies to the process of creating clay fabric).

Seed beads—a general term for very small glass beads. Sizes and finishes may vary.

Skinner blend—a color blending technique in polymer clay developed by Judith Skinner. It involves combining triangles of several colors of clay placed next to each other, which are then blended to fade from one color to the next by using a folding and rolling process and a pasta machine.

Split ring—a small double metal loop of wire used for securely connecting components in jewelry making.

Stippling—a painting technique involving dabbing a brush or sponge coated with one color of paint over another color to create a mottled effect.

Terra cotta—defined as 'baked earth,' terra cotta is a reddish brown type of clay often used to create earthenware, tiles, and decorative objects, and it is often glazed (it also refers to Sculpey polymer clay in the color and texture of terra cotta).

Tissue blade—a very thin rectangular steel blade with a sharp edge that was originally developed for medical purposes. It is excellent for slicing solid polymer clay (variations include the Sculpey Super Slicer and the Kato NuBlade).

Transfer—refers to a the action of applying a photocopied (with toner), laser printed, or glossy magazine image to either solid or liquid polymer clay.

Varnish—a clear gloss or matte finish applied as a finishing coat to a polymer clay project. It must be a finish that is compatible with polymer clay. Fimo varnish is one of the best choices. Spray finishes are not recommended.

Veneer—a thin layer of colored or patterned polymer clay that can be applied to the surface of a project made of polymer clay or other bakeable materials for a decorative look.

Wire clippers—a small hand-held tool with cutting blades specifically used for cutting thin wire in jewelry making (available in large sizes for thick wire).

Resources

AUTHORS

Ann and Karen Mitchell
AnKara Designs
(626) 798-8491
www.ankaradesigns.com
ankara@ankaradesigns.com
(jewelry and craft designers and teachers)

DISTRIBUTORS

Accent Import Export Inc.
1501 Loveridge Rd. Box 16
Pittsburg, CA 94565
(800) 989-2889
www.fimozone.com
(metallic leaf, Fimo varnish)

Amaco—American Art Clay Co., Inc.
4717 W. 16th St.
Indianapolis, IN 46222
(800) 374-1600
www.amaco.com
(Friendly Clay stamps, ArtEmboss craft foil,
leaf and shape cutters)

American Science & Surplus
P.O. Box 1030
Skokie, IL 60076
(847) 647-0011
www.sciplus.com
(aluminum boxes with glass-lidded canisters)

The Art Store
13 store locations
(888) 546-2787
www.artstore.com
(oil paints—Art Store, Van Gogh, Grumbacher,
Winsor, and Newton brands; brushes; brush
cleaner; wooden tools; clay tools; X-acto
and craft knives)

The Clay Factory
P.O. Box 460598
Escondido, CA 92046-0598
(877) Sculpey or (877) 728-5739
www.clayfactoryinc.com
(Liquid Sculpey, Premo, Sculpey III, Shapelets,
Atlas pasta machines, tissue blades, Pearl
Ex mica pigment powders, Kemper tools)

FlexiClay Corp.
5615 Foxwood, Suite C
Oak Park, CA 91377
www.FlexiClay.com
(rubber FlexiClay for molding)

Joann Fabric, Craft, and Home stores
(888) 739-4120 for store locations
www.joann.com
(fabrics, trim, Velcro hook and loop fasteners,
eyelets and eyelet setting tool)

Michaels Stores, Inc.
850 North Lake Dr.
Suite 500
Coppell, TX 75019
(800) Michaels or (800) 642-4235
www.michaels.com
(general craft products, glass items, vase,
votive, adhesives—E-6000, 527, rhinestones,
brushes, brush cleaner, some clay tools,
acrylic rollers, embossing powders,
embossing heat tool, glitters, wooden
boxes, metal palettes, picture frame glass,
clear elastic, decorative punches,
rhinestones and cabochons, clock
movement, 3M wet/dry sanding sponge,
ruler, leather supplies, Fiskars cutting tools)

**Polymer Clay Express at The Art Way
Studio**
13017 Wisteria Drive
P.O. Box 275
Germantown, MD 20874
(301) 482-0435
(800) 844-0138
www.polymerclayexpress.net
(Ateco cutters, assorted polymer clay
supplies)

Powdered Pearls
(877) 631-8028
www.powderedpearls.com
(mica pigment powders)

Prairiecraft
P.O. Box 209
Florissant, CO 80816-0209
(800) 779-0615
www.prairiecraft.com
(Kato Clear Polyclay Medium, Kato Poly Clay,
Kato Nublade, Kato clay tools, metallic leaf)

Rings and Things
P.O. Box 450
Spokane, WA 99210-0450
(800) 366-2156
www.rings-things.com
(jewelry findings, barrettes, beads,
rhinestones, Fimo gloss varnish, jewelry
making tools, clear elastic, GS cement glue,
wire, Beadalon, crimp beads)

Stamp Happy
890 Mission Ridge Dr.
Manteca, CA 95337
www.stamp-happy.com
(rubber stamps)

MAGAZINES

Bead and Button
Kalmbach Publishing Company
21027 Crossroads Circle
P.O. Box 1612
Waukesha, WI 53187
(800) 533-6644
www.beadandbutton.com

Belle Armoire
Stampington and Company
22992 Mill Creek, Suite B
Laguna Hills, CA 92653
(949) 380-7318
www.bellearmoire.com

MANUFACTURERS

Art Institute Glitter, Inc.
The Art Glittering System
720 N. Balboa Street
Cottonwood, AZ 86326
(877) 909-0805
www.artglitter.com
(glitter)

Fiskars Brands, Inc.
School, Office, and Craft Division
7811 West Stewart Avenue
Wausau, WI 54401
(800) 950-0203
(715) 842-2091
www.fiskarsbrands.com
(scissors, cutting tools, decorative scissors)

Kemper Tools
13595 12th St.
Chino, CA 91710
(800) 388-5367
www.kempertools.com
(cutters, polymer clay tools)

The Leather Factory
P.O. Box 50429
Fort Worth, TX 76105
(800) 433-3201
(817) 496-4414
www.leatherfactory.com
(leather stamps, eyelet punch and setter,
mallet, pad, Tanner's Bond Craftsman
contact cement)

Polyform Products
1901 Estes Ave.
Elk Grove, IL 60007
(847) 427-0426
www.sculpey.com
(Liquid Sculpey, Premo, Sculpey III, cutters,
Shapelets, texture sheets)

Rupert, Gibbon & Spider Incorporated
P.O. Box 425
Healdsburg, CA
(800) 442-0455
www.jacquardproducts.com
(Pearl-ex mica pigment powders)

Stampendous!, Inc.
1240 N. Red Gum
Anaheim, CA 92806-1820
(800) 869-0474
(714) 688-0288
www.stampendous.com
(stamping and scrapbooking supplies)

US Artquest
7800 Ann Arbor Rd.
Grass Lake, MI 49240
(517) 522-6225
www.usartquest.com
(Gildenglitz variegated metallic leaf)

Walnut Hollow Farm, Inc.
1409 State Road 23
Dodgeville, WI 53533
(800) 950-5101
www.walnuthollow.com
(clock movement, oil based colored pencils,
decorative unfinished wood items)

Expression
Publishers' Development Corp.
591 Camino de la Reina, Suite 200
San Diego, CA 92108
(619) 819-4520
www.expressionartmagazine.com

Jewelry Crafts
Miller Magazines
4880 Market St.
Ventura, CA 93003
(800) 784-5709
www.jewelrycrafts.com

Ornament
P.O. Box 2349
San Marcos, CA 92079-2349
(800) 888-8950

PolymerCAFÉ Magazine
4640 Nantucket Drive
Lilburn GA, 30047
www.polymercafe.com

BOOKS

Broschart and Braun, *Ornamental Designs from Architectural Sheet Metal*, Mineola, NY: The Athanaeum of Philadelphia and Dover Publications, Inc, 1992.

Classic Clip Art, New York: Glorya Hale Books, Random House Value Publishing, Inc., 1996.

Grafton, Carol Belanger (ed.), *Floral Motifs for Designers, Needleworkers*, and Craftspeople, Mineola, NY: Dover Publications, Inc., 1986.

———*Floral Ornament*, Mineola, NY: Dover Publications, Inc., 1997.

———*Victorian Floral Illustrations*, Mineola, NY: Dover Publications, Inc., 1985.

Heaser, Sue, *The Polymer Clay Techniques Book*, Cincinnati: North Light Books, 1999.

Knight, F., *700 Victorian Ornamental Designs*, Mineola, NY: Dover Publications, Inc., 1998.

Leighton, John, *1,100 Designs and Motifs from Historic Sources*, New York: Dover Publications, Inc., 1995.

McGuire, Barbara A., *Creative Stamping in Polymer Clay*, Cincinnati: North Light Books, 2002.

———*Foundations in Polymer Clay Design*, Iola, Wis.: Krause Publications, 1999.

Roche, Nan, *The New Clay*, Rockville, MD: Flower Valley Press, 1991.

Roessing, H., *2,286 Traditional Stencil Designs*, Mineola, NY, The Athanaeum of

Philadelphia and Dover Publications, Inc., 1991.

Sibbet, Jr., Ed, *Art Nouveau Designs*, Mineola, NY: Dover Publications, Inc., 1981.

Spero, James (edited by), *Decorative Patterns from Historic Sources*, Mineola, NY: 1986.

PUBLISHERS

Dover Publications, Inc.
31 East 2nd Street
Mineola, NY 11501
store.doverpublications.com

Glorya Hale Books
Random House Value Publishing, Inc.
201 East 50th Street
New York, NY 10022
www.randomhouse.com

Krause Publications
700 E. State St.
Iola, WI 54990-0001
(715) 445-2214
www.krause.com

ORGANIZATIONS

National Polymer Clay Guild
PMB 345
1350 Beverly Road, 115
McLean, VA 22101
www.npcg.org

Bibliography

BOOKS

Dubin, Lois Sherr, *The History of Beads:* From 30,000 B.C. to the Present. New York: Harry N. Abrams, Inc., 1987.

Gabriel, Jeanette Hanisee, *The Gilbert Collection Micromosaics*. London: Philip Wilson Publishers, 2000.

Janson, H. W., *History of Art*. New York: Harry N. Abrams, Inc., 1986.

Jones, Owen, *The Grammar of Ornament*. New York: DK Publishing, Inc., 2001.

Marascutto, Pauline B., Mario Stainer, and Perle Veneziane. *Nuove Edizini Polomiti*. S.r.l.: 1991.

Webster's Encyclopedia Unabridged Dictionary of the English Language, New York: Portland House, 1989.

WEB SITES

members.nccw.net
palimpsest.stanford.edu
www.Bartleby.com
www.thecameocollection.com
www.encyclopedia.com
www.greekmosaics.com
www.houstoncul.org
www.ive.org.uk
www.panicosm.com
www.suminagashi.com

Notes

[1] Janson, H. W., History of Art, (N.Y.: Harry N. Abrams, Inc. 1986), pages 9-11.

[2] Webster's Encyclopedia Unabridged Dictionary of the English Language (New York: Portland House, 1989) page 711, 1229.

[3] Janson, pages 26-27.

[4] Janson, pages 54-55.

[5] Janson, pages 194-195.

[6] www.thecameocollection.com

[7] Jones, Owen, The Grammar of Ornament, (New York: DK Publishing, Inc., 2001) pages 48, 56.

[8] Jones, page 102.

[9] Jones, page 130.

[10] Jones, page 295.

[11] Jones, page 252.

[12] www.greekmosaics.com.

[13] www.greekmosaics.com.

[14] Janson, page 190.

[15] Janson, pages 243-244.

[16] www. Bartleby.com.

[17] www. Bartleby.com.

[18] Gabriel, Jeanette Hanisee, The Gilbert Collection Micromosaics, (London: Philip Wilson Publishers, 2000) pages 11-13.

[19] Gabriel, page 16.

[20] www.encyclopedia.com.

[21] www.encyclopedia.com.

[22] palimpsest.stanford.edu

[23] www.suminagashi.com from Maurer, Diane, Marbling: A Complete Guide to Creating Beautiful Patterned Papers and Fabrics, (New York: Friedman/Fairfax Publishers, 1959)

[24] www.suminagashi.com

[25] members.nccw.net

[26] Dubin, Lois Sherr, The History of Beads, from 30,000B.C. To the Present, (New York: Harry N. Abrams, Inc. 1987) page 43

[27] Dubin, page 48

[28] Dubin, pages 158-159

[29] Dubin, page 93

[30] Dubin, page 107

[31] Dubin, pages 110-111

[32] Marascutto, Pauline B. and Mario Stainer, "Perle Veneziane," (Verona: Nuove Edizioni Dolomiti S.r.l. 1991) page 94

[33] www.ive.org.uk

[34] www.panicosm.com

[35] www.ive.org.uk

[36] www.ive.org.uk

[37] www.ive.org.uk

[38] www.ive.org.uk

[39] www.houstoncul.org

[40] www.thestorefinder.com/glass/glass/history.html

[41] Janson, page 339

[42] www.thestorefinder.com/glass/glass/history.html

[43] www.thestorefinder.com/glass/glass/history.html

Index

Above: This beautiful purse is comprised of clay fabric transfer elements appliquéd over and under the silk organza backing. The transfers have been further enhanced with painted dots of liquid clay. The purse is decorated with polymer clay bead handle and drops.

Left: This decorative shirt is machine stitched and made entirely from transfer clay fabric. The transfers were designed from two photographs of an Indian window and a palace detail. The neckline is enhanced with liquid clay fabric lace.

About the Authors

Ann and Karen Mitchell have been working in polymer clay for more than 15 years. Over the last four years, they have been developing new techniques in liquid polymer clay. Their distinctive designs have appeared in feature films, television, theatrical productions, and museum exhibitions. The sisters have made numerous guest appearances on television including "The Carol Duvall Show" on HGTV. They continue to write articles for magazines, and teach their techniques at polymer clay conferences. Their elegant and feminine jewelry can be seen in a number of art and craft books. Their innovative pieces have appeared in several ads for Polyform Products. Ann and Karen established their company, AnKara Designs, in 1991, and specialize in creating and marketing their extensive collection of mixed media jewelry and accessories.

Ann and Karen Mitchell

About the Photographer

Cristopher Lapp

Cristopher Lapp's photography is a celebration of beauty from every corner of the earth. Although he is a versatile, sought-after "commercial" photographer, his images are best described as "fine art". Hollywood's elite, including Michael Jackson and Elton John, collect his work.

Cristopher's credits range from magazine ads in *Vogue, GQ, W, National Geographic, Better Homes & Gardens* and *Sunset Magazine* to a calendar for the Huntington Library, Art Collections, and Botanical Gardens in San Marino, California. His work can be viewed at www.cristopherlapp.com.